☑ THE CHECKLIST SERIES

MANAGING OPERATIONS

Chartered
Management
Institute

PROFILE BOOKS

First published in Great Britain in 2015 by
Profile Books Ltd
3 Holford Yard
Bevin Way
London WC1X 9HD
www.profilebooks.com

10 9 8 7 6 5 4 3 2 1

A CIP catalogue record for this book is available from the British Library.

ISBN: 978 1 78125 220 8
eISBN: 978 1 78283 032 0

Text design by sue@lambledesign.demon.co.uk

Typeset in Helvetica by MacGuru Ltd
info@macguru.org.uk

Printed and bound in Britain by Clays, Bungay, Suffolk

FSC
www.fsc.org
MIX
Paper from
responsible sources
FSC® C018072

MANAGING
OPERATIONS

About the checklist series

Management can be a daunting task. Managers are expected to provide direction, foster commitment, facilitate change and achieve results through the efficient, creative and responsible deployment of people and other resources. On top of that, managers have to manage themselves and develop their own personal skills. Just keeping up is a challenge – and we cannot be experts in everything.

The checklists in this series have been developed over many years by the Chartered Management Institute (CMI) to meet this challenge by addressing the main issues that managers can expect to face during their career. Each checklist distils good practice from industry to provide a clear and straightforward overview of a specific topic or activity, and has been reviewed by CMI's Subject Matter Experts Panel to reflect new research and changes in working life.

The series is designed both for managers who need an introduction to unfamiliar topics, and for those who want to refresh their understanding of the salient points. In more specialised areas – for example, financial management – checklists can also enable the generalist manager to work more effectively with experts, or to delegate more effectively to a subordinate.

Why is the checklist format useful? Checklists provide a logical, structured framework to help professional managers deal with an increasingly complex workplace – they help shape our thoughts and save us from being confused by too much information. At the same time, checklists help us to make good use of what we already know. They help us to remember things and prevent us from forgetting something important. Thus, no matter how expert we may already be, using checklists can improve outcomes and give us the confidence to manage more effectively, and to get the job done.

About this book

This book is aimed at anyone who is looking for an introduction to how organisational activities can be managed efficiently, avoiding waste of time and resources and unnecessary duplication of effort.

The search for quality has led to the development of a range of techniques for ensuring the maintenance of high standards in business operations. A combination of action-oriented checklists and short summaries of the work of seminal management thinkers will guide you through the basics of such tools, from total quality management to lean management. The book also covers essential skills needed by managers in what many are calling a VUCA world, characterised by volatility, uncertainty, complexity and ambiguity: the ability to participate in and manage projects and programmes of change effectively; an understanding of how to assess and manage risk; and the know-how to plan for potential disruptions to business.

A further section focuses on the supply chain and covers topics such as purchasing, inventory management, outsourcing, service level agreements and invitations to tender.

Contents

The supply chain

Monitoring and control

Introduction

Whatever your specialisation, a basic understanding of operations will be important as you progress in your career. Effective operations are at the core of virtually every organisation's activities. This book will introduce you to the key elements of operations management and provide you with practical advice on what to do – and what to avoid.

Operations translate the vision and business strategy of an organisation into reality: to do this well, efficient and effective execution is key. If you aim to reach the top of an organisation, it will give you a considerable advantage if you can demonstrate that you have successfully managed, and continuously improved, operations at an earlier stage in your career.

What do we mean by 'operations management'? Maintaining, controlling, and improving the organisational activities that are required to produce goods or services for consumers is a core management function. All types of operations have certain common characteristics: they all have inputs, they all transform those inputs through different processes, and they all have outputs. The processes all use resources, which are created, managed, improved, re-engineered and eventually replaced. Businesses look for ways to reduce waste and lower resource use as a means to gain efficiencies and improve the financial health of the organisation, including the application of ISO 9001 quality systems, or total quality management techniques; they may also need to design and create new operations to launch a new product or service.

Historically, operations management has been associated with specific sectors such as manufacturing, retail or infrastructure services. Perhaps unfairly, operations are often seen as dull – the daily grind of getting things done consistently and well. It is easy to form a false impression that operations are just about making slow, incremental improvements to long-established processes.

In recent years the importance of operations management has increasingly been recognised. This reflects on the one hand an acknowledgement that operations are vital to a business's competitiveness and sustainability, and on the other the rise of interest in 'green' policies and concerns over the environment. In addition, improving productivity improves the financial health of a business during difficult economic conditions. The business environment is increasingly volatile, uncertain, complex and ambiguous, so operations managers have to cope with constant change. Change comes in many forms: major competition, shorter product and service life cycles, better educated and quality-conscious consumers, and the capabilities of new technology. Fundamentally, operations management can help a business to meet its customers' priorities. The operations manager has to find ways to improve productivity while providing a broad array of high-quality products and services.

To be a successful operations manager, you will have to lead change and communicate the reasons behind it, as well as having to learn how to apply the techniques of operations management to ensure the changes deliver the benefits they are supposed to do. This book will help you to think about the key elements of operations management: about how to manage change and undertake projects; how to manage quality and your supply chain; and how to monitor, control and improve your operations. These are skills which will be valuable whether you stay in operations or move into other management areas.

Gareth Rhys Williams

Gareth Rhys Williams started his management career in operations at Lucas Industries before moving into general management. He has been CEO of four businesses, most recently Charter International plc and PHS Group

Mapping an effective change programme

Managing change involves planning and carrying out actions designed to achieve a transition from the current situation in an organisation to a more desirable one in the future. It involves anticipating and minimising obstacles to achieving change as well as dealing with any problems that arise during the transition.

The scope of change management programmes can vary from continuous improvement initiatives, which involve small changes to existing processes, to radical and substantial changes in organisational structure and strategy. Change can be reactive, in response to events that have already taken place, or proactive, in response to anticipated conditions in the future. It may be triggered by changes in an organisation's external environment, for example in the economic, commercial or political arenas; or it may be in response to perceived weaknesses within the organisation, for example its internal processes and structures.

In turbulent and uncertain times change has become a fact of everyday organisational life. It is seen as normal, continuous and prevalent; it cannot be sidestepped or avoided. At times, change can be a relatively painless evolutionary process of adapting to circumstances, but in many cases more dramatic and far-reaching change is necessary, if businesses are to improve performance, deliver added value and remain competitive. Organisational change programmes, which ask people to do different things or to do things differently and call for radical shifts in attitudes and behaviour, are challenging for both the employees who have to take change on board and the managers who have to plan and manage the change process. It cannot be denied that change is frequently painful, but individuals and organisations need to learn how to handle it if they are to survive.

A study carried out by Towers Watson, a professional services firm, in 2013 found that 55% of all change programmes fail. This highlights how important it is for managers to take a considered approach to the introduction of change, and in particular to take account of human reactions to change as well as the organisational and procedural issues involved. Individuals may feel threatened by change, particularly when they have no control over it, but they will cope better if they have some involvement or influence in the process and some degree of ability to control its pace and direction. Uncertainty about position, status or financial livelihood can cause individuals to feel stressed and fearful. This can lead to resistance and obstructive behaviour or a premature decision to leave the organisation. Managers who can anticipate problems of this nature and have the skills and experience to motivate people and involve them in planning and implementing change are more likely to be successful in keeping their organisations competitive and effective.

Change programmes come in many different shapes and sizes and may involve the use of specific quality management standards and systems, ranging from total quality management to lean management practices and Six Sigma. This checklist outlines a generic process for the introduction of change and considers what factors managers must take into account when planning change programmes.

Action checklist

1 Think through the need for change

Take the time to think through why change is needed and what kind of change is required. What has triggered the need for change? Is it a result of external or internal factors? How urgent is the need for change? This will assist you in making the case for change later.

At this initial stage you may find it helpful to read a book by a recognised expert to raise your awareness of the issues involved in change management, such as John Kotter's *A Force for Change* or Rosabeth Moss Kanter's *The Change Masters*. Time invested in getting a broader perspective can bring ample rewards and could help you to avoid costly mistakes.

2 Define the scope of change

It is important to define the scope of the change programme rigorously, if it is to be effective.

Consider the following:

- Will the changes involve a fundamental rethink of the purpose of the organisation and what its strategy should be?
- Is it a matter of restructuring or downsizing?
- Is there a need to update systems and processes?
- Will the whole organisation be affected or will the changes be limited to particular departments or functions?
- Is the organisation looking to introduce new ways of working?
- Are new skills needed or are there new tasks that must be carried out?
- How will job roles and responsibilities be affected?
- Will training be required?
- Who will be affected most?

Six areas that should be considered in any major change initiative are:

- markets and customers
- products and services
- business processes
- people and reward systems

- structure and facilities
- technology.

3 Build the case for change

You may now have a clear understanding of why the organisation needs to change, but you will need to convince others. Persuading people of the need for change is a complex and sensitive business, and it may be awkward if the need for change appears to have come out of the blue. Consider whether it could be helpful to bring someone in from outside the organisation to act as a catalyst, but manage this with care and sensitivity if you decide to go ahead.

Drawing on the reasons for change identified earlier, draw up a clear business case that marshals quantitative and qualitative arguments linked to the achievement of business objectives. Bear in mind that most change programmes are costly, and ambitious targets will almost certainly need to be set if there is to be a reasonable return on investment. Set out a clear vision of the organisation's position once the changes have been made and the benefits that will be derived from successful implementation. Cover the implications of the changes for organisational structures and culture: will you be moving from a hierarchical to a team-based culture, for example? And what impact will this have on the organisation?

4 Consider the human factors

Think carefully about who will be most affected by the proposed changes and consider how they are likely to react. Change often evokes emotional responses, so be ready to listen and respond to any objections and concerns that are raised.

Consider, too, how you can motivate people to get involved in the change process and take ownership of it. It may be possible to ask employees to identify change factors for themselves, so that they will gain insight into the need for change. In all events, the rationale for change must be clearly explained and the benefits communicated to everyone involved. This should help to reduce uncertainty, allay fears and minimise resistance to change. Research has shown that employees who participate actively in change programmes experience a sense of meaningfulness in their work and higher levels of job satisfaction. Employees who feel disempowered, however, are more likely to become disengaged and dissatisfied.

Ways to build commitment include:

- sharing information as widely as possible (within the constraints of confidentiality) and minimising surprises
- allowing people to make suggestions, give input and express differences of opinion
- breaking change down into manageable chunks or projects
- making standards and requirements clear and ensuring they are understood
- being honest about any difficulties or downsides.

5 Build a culture that supports change

Organisational culture plays an important role in supporting change. A supportive culture can be developed by:

- recognising prevailing values and beliefs
- creating a climate where people feel safe to raise issues or ask questions
- breaking down departmental barriers
- designing challenging jobs
- freeing up time for creative thinking and innovation
- focusing on the interests of all stakeholders.

Methods of handling people issues include:

- recognising staff needs and dealing with conflict positively and openly
- giving clear direction without being directive

- involving everyone in change
- earning the commitment and trust of all stakeholders
- developing relationships between team members
- understanding how teams work
- recognising the talents and limitations of individuals.

6 Gain the commitment of senior management

Senior managers need to be fully committed to change programmes if they are to be successful. Establish from the outset whether the management team is signed up to change, and address the position of those who are not enthusiastic supporters honestly. Make sure that senior managers are included among those consulted when proposing change.

7 Appoint a champion for change

It can be immensely helpful for a senior person to champion the changes. Change programmes benefit from a lead person who drives the plan forward and galvanises people into action. This should not necessarily be the same person as the change programme manager. Often the two roles of programme manager and business change manager are kept separate: the former is responsible for facilitating and delivering change; the latter is responsible for realising the business benefits of change by working across the boundary between the change programme and the wider organisation. The business change manager is often supported by a network of change champions reaching into all parts of the business.

8 Build the right team to manage the changes

Select a team with a mix of technical competencies, personal styles and levels of seniority. Team members should be respected individuals from within the organisation, rather than outsiders. You need movers and shakers whose commitment is not in doubt, but it is useful to temper the mix with a few known critics. All should have earned respect within the organisation and be widely trusted and credible.

9 Draw up an outline plan

Plan for change in the way you would for any major project. Break the change down into its component parts and map the change processes that will be needed. If change is to be successful, the plan must be well defined and focus clearly on the objectives to be achieved.

The following elements should be covered:

- **Vision.** What is the big idea behind the change? What is the organisation striving to achieve? This must be expressed in a clear and compelling manner.

- **Scope.** What needs to change if the organisation is to realise its vision?

- **Time frame.** What will change when, and in what order? Radical change takes time, especially if a change in attitude is involved.

- **Organisation structure.** Will changes be needed, for example towards a flatter structure?

- **People.** Who will be most affected by change and how? Who will play prominent roles in implementing change (the change agents)?

- **Resources.** How much will the change cost? Will there be offsetting benefits?

- **Controls.** What controls will be in place to ensure that the change progresses satisfactorily?

- **Communications.** Will you need new mechanisms and structures to communicate with frontline employees?

- **Training.** Have time and resources been allocated for the training of managers and frontline employees in both the hard and soft skills associated with change?

10 Cost the change programme

Change is costly, particularly when it is associated with plant closure or redundancies. Recognise this and draw up a separate budget. Do not underestimate the softer costs of training, or the communications the programme will require.

11 Identify driving and restraining forces

In any organisation, there will be forces driving change and forces hindering change; you need to identify both. Plan to reinforce the drivers, or add new ones, and to weaken or lessen the restraining forces through communication and education. This will usually be a slow process, but it can be helped by frank discussion, and even more by positive success.

12 Outline the change programme to line managers

Outline the reasons for and the potential benefits of the proposed changes to line managers. Explain the likely impact of the programme on structures, people, processes and products. Seek feedback and use it to refine the plan and build consensus in favour of change.

13 Communicate

Communication is the key to successful change. Communicate continuously with stakeholders – employees, customers, suppliers and owners – as you plan and build the programme. Be honest with employees about the likely extent of change and the potential effects on them. Do not allow rumours to circulate: pre-empt them through frank, open and timely communications and discussion.

14 Identify change agents

Although change is usually initiated from the top, and led by a change team, it needs to be promoted and pushed through by change champions. These should be the organisation's own employees, not external consultants. Select people who are

committed and enthusiastic, and who can command respect.
Make plans to train them to help in leading and cascading the
change programme throughout the organisation.

As a manager you should avoid:

- forgetting that change management needs to have a vision, a
  purpose, a rationale, a direction and a time frame
- forgetting to engage with and listen to your staff
- overlooking the need to celebrate and reward success – people
  need to feel good about their achievements, however big or small
- thinking small – many change programmes fail to deliver the
  expected results because their ambitions are too narrow, or not
  radical enough
- failing to take account of external stakeholders – seek the views
  of customers, suppliers and other stakeholder groups as well as
  those within the organisation
- expecting rapid change – be patient and persistent, as change
  takes time
- underestimating the cost of change – build in costings for
  continuing communication and training
- embarking on a major change programme without the absolute
  support of the top management team
- riding roughshod over resistance to change – instead listen and
  persuade.

Implementing an effective change programme

Managing change involves accomplishing a transition from position A to position B and handling any problems that arise. The process of change within organisations usually results from interactions between four major elements: equipment (technology); processes (working procedures); organisation structure; people. Change in any one of these will inevitably lead to changes in the others, as organisations are complex interrelated systems.

The ability to manage change effectively is a key managerial skill in a society where rapid change has become the norm and new technologies are continually being introduced. However, research shows that many, if not most, change efforts fail to achieve their objectives, at least to some extent. Paying close attention to the process of implementation will pay dividends in terms of your ability to achieve objectives and achieve and sustain organisational success.

Change management can be a slow, painful and expensive process. An informed and thoughtful approach is needed to address both hard logistical issues and softer people issues. Many people find change difficult and may resist or try to hinder the process. A combination of patience and firmness will help managers to handle change programmes effectively, especially where they are seeking to change attitudes and behaviour.

The detailed schedule for implementing change will vary according to the type of organisation and the nature and scope of the changes that are planned. There are, however, common issues that should be considered and general principles that should be followed when introducing change, regardless of the specific context. Many different models are used for managing change. Managers may wish to study the ideas of writers such as John Kotter, Rosabeth Moss Kanter, Kurt Lewin and Bernard Burnes and identify a model that they feel will work well in their particular situation.

This checklist aims to provide some generic guidance for those implementing change in their organisation. It assumes that a sound business case for change has been made, and that the scope and objectives of the change have been clearly defined and carefully thought through.

Action checklist

1 Agree the implementation strategy

Before you begin to embark on a change programme, you must have a clear strategy based on the objectives and outline plans that have already been set. The details of the implementation will depend on the desired outcomes and on the approach to be taken, whether this is to be top-down, bottom-up, or a mix of both. Decide also whether to introduce change by division, by department, or throughout the organisation. Bear in mind that a big-bang approach is not normally advisable, as most organisations have only a finite capacity to cope with change. When deciding which approach to take, it is also important to think about where the key influencers are and how communication channels will work.

A programme of change is unlikely to be the only corporate initiative under way at any given time. Ensure that the strategy and goals behind the programme are consistent with those of other organisational initiatives, and that all are pointing in the same direction. Make sure that employees receive consistent messages about the organisation's core values and beliefs in relation to all the initiatives.

2 Agree time frames

Every change programme needs a start date. You should also aim to set a finite time frame for the implementation, regardless of whether it is being introduced incrementally or simultaneously across all divisions. The timetable must be stretching enough to convey urgency, but attainable enough to be motivating and realistic.

3 Draw up detailed implementation plans

Draw up detailed implementation plans with each divisional or departmental head in line with both the strategy and timetable that have been agreed. The team responsible for the changes can act as a source of advice and consultancy when necessary, but line managers should be empowered to determine how to implement the change in their areas of responsibility, in accordance with its overall goals. For senior management, decide how progress will be monitored and whether stage reviews are necessary.

4 Set up a team of change champions

The change champion team will not necessarily include senior management, but it will benefit from a board-level champion. The team should include the key people involved in designing and delivering the change, as well as those affected by it. This team has an important role to play in benefits realisation management – defining and disseminating the benefits of the changes and communicating them effectively in their own parts of the organisation.

5 Establish good programme management practices

Treat change in the same way as any project or programme. Consider using a recognised project or programme management tool or methodology, such as Managing Successful Programmes (MSP). Keep objectives in mind, set milestones and monitor progress to keep the programme on schedule and on budget.

Do not assume that change will be wholly successful or painless. Undertake a risk analysis and make any necessary contingency plans. It is imperative to flag up potential problems as early as possible. Also keep track of the costs associated with implementing change and ensure that a contingency budget is in place. Establish ground rules for the programme team, particularly with regard to information-sharing, decision-making and reporting.

6 Communicate clearly

The importance of good communications to the success of change programmes cannot be underestimated. Good communications should be based on careful stakeholder analysis to ensure the right messages get to the right stakeholders through the best channels. Identify your stakeholders, map them carefully, and then communicate with each stakeholder group in a manner that will encourage their positive engagement with the aims of the programme.

Do all you can to ensure that employees at every level of the organisation understand the reasons for change and know what will be happening, when it will be happening and what is expected of them. Often it is uncertainty rather than change that really worries employees. Provide as much information as possible and quash inaccurate rumours as soon as they arise.

Do not assume that everything is clear to everyone after a single message. Communication should be constant. Provide opportunities for employees to seek clarification where necessary, and give regular updates and progress reports. Be sure to report on early wins and celebrate successes.

7 Ensure participation and help to minimise stress

All change is stressful, and it can be especially stressful if it is imposed without consultation or adequate communication. This can have a detrimental effect on how well change is adopted and sustained in the longer term. There are, of course, instances when change has to be imposed to address an issue such as a financial crisis, but mechanisms can be introduced to facilitate the process. Fear of the unknown rather than change itself is often a major stress factor, but its impact can be reduced if you are as open as possible about the consequences of change.

8 Personalise the case for change

Individual employees must feel they can take ownership of the change programme as it evolves. This is much easier when they can personalise it and relate it to their own work and team. Ensure that line managers are able to present the corporate case for change in terms that every individual in the company can relate to. Consider what change will mean for each individual in terms of status (job title, budget responsibility); habits (changes to working time, new colleagues); beliefs and attitudes (move to a customer focus); and behaviour (new working practices). Changes to working practices will need input from the HR department at the planning stage and may require specific change activity or union consultation, for example.

9 Be prepared for conflict and manage it effectively

Change usually results in conflict of one kind or another, simply because people have different views and react to stressful situations in different ways. Try to bring conflict to the surface rather than allow it to fester; tackle it by examining and analysing it with those involved and seeking ways to resolve the issues. Conflict can often be put to positive use. For example, open discussion and clarification can lead to the resolution of difficulties and the introduction of improvements.

When conflict cannot be resolved through explanation and discussion, you will have to negotiate and persuade. This means avoiding getting into an entrenched position yourself, and working out how to influence others if they dig their heels in too deeply. It also means finding ways to reach agreement on the best way forward without major loss of face for either side, while at the same time trying not to prejudice the underlying change initiative.

10 Motivate your employees

Sustained change requires high levels of motivation, and this will be difficult without strong relationships of trust and respect across the organisation. Recognise that employees need to feel valued, to have their efforts and achievements recognised, and to be developed and challenged. Be aware that different people are motivated by different types of reward.

11 Develop skills

View the change programme as a learning process. Give attention to developing both technical and interpersonal skills at all levels within the organisation and integrate this into corporate training and development programmes. Specific training to enable change, such as providing an induction into new systems and technologies, may also be needed.

Change also provides an opportunity to develop learning capability and build a culture of learning into the organisation. Creating goals and plans that everyone can subscribe to will enable everyone to benefit. Turn learning into something that people want to buy into, rather than a chore – help people feel the buzz of discovery and involvement in new developments. Set an example by updating the skills of senior management.

12 Maintain momentum

Incremental change is often a long process, consisting of small and often imperceptible changes in behaviour and attitudes. Accept that change may be a stop/start process. Watch out for signs that initial enthusiasm is flagging and the pace of change is slowing to an unacceptable rate. Plan for this and develop strategies to create a sense of purpose and urgency and give fresh impetus. To gear the organisation up for renewed efforts after setbacks, seek innovative ways to remind staff of the overall case for change and reinforce its value to them. A set of quick wins and visible success points is a useful framework for achieving this. Leading indicators of potential benefits are also helpful in maintaining interest and demonstrating progress.

Think about how to address problems that have prevented progress in the past. Ask yourself what and who is preventing progress, and who can help to unblock the situation. Your analysis of stakeholder groups, and of their varying interests and perspectives (as mentioned in point 6 above), should help you gain an understanding of the forces in play. Aim to break the code of silence that engenders organisational protectionism and maintains the status quo.

13 Monitor and evaluate

Monitor and evaluate the results of the change programme against the goals and milestones established in the original plan. Are these goals still appropriate or do they need to be revised in the light of experience? Existing performance measures may not be compatible with the changes being introduced and may hinder change unless they are revised. Check that all the measures used are consistent with organisational vision and goals, and if not redesign them. Be honest in your assessment of progress. If there is a real divergence between the planned goals and reality, admit this and take corrective action without delay. Be open about failure and involve employees in setting new targets or devising new measures.

In some circumstances it may be necessary to engage an internal or external change agent as they will have the skills and abilities needed to facilitate a difficult process of change. Organisations that are otherwise good at what they do may nonetheless find it difficult to manage change effectively.

As a manager you should avoid:

- trying to implement change without senior management sponsorship and commitment
- going ahead without involving employees at every stage of design and implementation
- failing to anticipate resistance or prepare for it

- forgetting to take implementation costs into account
- getting lost in the detail and losing sight of the vision
- failing to publicise successes to build up momentum and support.

Rosabeth Moss Kanter

Pioneer of empowerment and change management

Introduction

Rosabeth Moss Kanter (b. 1943) is a Harvard academic and consultant and is best known for her work on change management and innovation. Her 1983 book *The Change Masters* was named the most influential business book of the 20th century by the *Financial Times*. She is a prolific writer and on a wide range of topics including leadership, power, high-performance organisations and social issues.

Kanter views herself as a thought leader and developer of ideas. Much of her success is due to a combination of rigorous research, practical insights and experience, and an ability to communicate in a clear and concrete way.

She has received many accolades and awards. In 2001, she received the Academy of Management's Distinguished Career Award for her scholarly contributions to management knowledge, and in 2002 she was named Intelligent Community Visionary of the Year by the World Teleport Association. She received the Warren Bennis Award for Leadership Excellence and is on the *Times* list of the fifty most powerful women in the world.

Life and career

Kanter was born in Cleveland, Ohio, and attended the top women's academy, Bryn Mawr. She took her PhD at the University of Michigan and was associate professor of sociology at Brandeis University from 1966 to 1977. Between 1973 and 1974 she taught on the Organizational Behavior Program at Harvard and she was a fellow and visiting scholar at Harvard Law School between 1975 and 1976.

From 1977 to 1986, Kanter was professor of sociology and professor of organisational management at Yale, and from 1979 to 1986 a visiting professor at Sloan School of Management, Massachusetts Institute of Technology (MIT). In 1986, she returned to Harvard as the 'class of 1960' professor of entrepreneurship and innovation.

Between 1989 and 1992 Kanter was editor of *Harvard Business Review*, and she acted as an economic adviser to Michael Dukakis during his 1988 presidential campaign. She has travelled widely as a public speaker, lecturer and international consultant. In 1977, she and her future husband, Barry Stein, set up a management consultancy, Goodmeasure, which has some large and well-known multinational companies, such as IBM, as clients.

Kanter currently holds the Ernest L Arbuckle professorship at Harvard Business School, specialising in strategy, innovation and leadership for change. She is also chair and director of the Harvard University Advanced Leadership Initiative, which assists leaders who have already been successful in their own working lives to use their leadership skills to tackle challenges in public services.

Publications

Kanter has authored or co-authored eighteen books and well over 150 major articles. Her doctoral thesis was on communes and her first books, written during the early 1970s, were sociological. The three books for which she is best known are *Men and Women of the Corporation*, *The Change Masters* and *When Giants Learn to Dance*. There is a logical progression within them: the first studies the stifling effects of bureaucratic organisation on individuals, and the second and third explore ways in which flatter, post-entrepreneurial organisations release, and make use of, individuals' talents and abilities. All three were successful and influential bestsellers.

Later books include *The Challenge of Organisational Change* (with Barry A Stein and Todd D Jick), *World Class: Thriving Locally in the Global Economy*, *The Frontiers of Management*, *Confidence* and *Supercorp*.

Men and Women of the Corporation

Men and Women of the Corporation (1977) won the C Wright Mills Award in 1977 as the year's best book on social issues. It is a detailed analysis of the nature and effects of the distribution of power and powerlessness within the headquarters of one large, bureaucratic, multinational corporation (called Industrial Supply Corporation, or Indsco, in the book). The effects of powerlessness on behaviour are explored and the detrimental effects of disempowerment, both for the organisation and individual employees, are made clear. Women were the most obvious group affected by lack of power, though Kanter emphasises that other groups outside the white, male norm, such as individuals from ethnic minorities, were also affected.

Three main structural variables explained the behaviours observed within Indsco:

- the structure of opportunity
- the structure of power
- the proportional distribution of people of different kinds.

Before this book was published, it was generally assumed that behavioural differences underlay women's general lack of career progress. Kanter's findings made structural issues central, however, and the implications for change management were significant. If all employees were to become more empowered, according to Kanter's analysis, organisations rather than people would need to change. Accordingly, the book ends with practical policy suggestions to create appropriate structural changes.

While working on this book, Kanter identified the need for organisational change to improve working life, create more equal opportunities and make more use of employees' talents within organisations.

The Change Masters

In *The Change Masters* (1983), approaches to achieving these ends are put forward. Kanter compares four traditional corporations like Indsco with six competitive and successful organisations, described as 'change masters'. All findings were weighed against the experiences of many other companies, and much other material. From the six innovative organisations, Kanter derives a model for encouraging innovation.

Innovative companies were found to have a distinct, 'integrative' approach to management; firms unlikely to innovate were described as 'segmentalist', being compartmentalised by units or departments. The difference begins with a company's approach to problem solving, and extends through its structure and culture. Entrepreneurial organisations:

- operate at the edge of their competence, focusing on exploring the unknown rather than on controlling the known
- measure themselves by future-focused visions (how far they have to go) rather than by past standards (how far they have come).

Three clusters of structures and processes are identified as factors that encourage power circulation and access to power: open communication systems, network-forming arrangements and decentralisation of resources. Their practical implementation is discussed.

Individuals can also be change masters. 'New entrepreneurs' are people who improve existing businesses rather than start new ones. They can be found in any functional area and are described as, literally, the right people, in the right place, at the right time:

- right people – vision and ideas extending beyond the organisation's normal practice

- right place – an integrative environment fostering proactive vision, coalitions and teams
- right time – moments in the historic flow when change becomes most possible.

The ultimate change masters are corporate leaders, who translate their vision into a new organisational reality.

The Change Masters advocates 'participation management' as the means to greater empowerment. Some major building blocks for productive change are identified, and practical measures to remove roadblocks to innovation are discussed.

When Giants Learn to Dance

When Giants Learn to Dance (1989) completes Kanter's trilogy on the need for change, which, she considered, US corporations had to confront and manage so as to compete more effectively. The book is based on observation from within various organisations, through consultancy projects. The global economy is likened to a 'corporate Olympics' of competing businesses, with results determining which nations, as well as which organisations, are winners.

The games differ, but successful teams share some characteristics such as strength, skill, discipline, good organisation and focus on individual excellence. To win, US companies will have to become progressively more entrepreneurial and less bureaucratic. The 'post-entrepreneurial' corporation is put forward as a model for the 1990s, fostered by the three shaping forces of:

- context set at the top
- top management values
- project ideas and approaches coming up through the organisation.

Such an 'athletic' organisation is lean, flexible and able to do more with less, and seeks to create synergies through the use of team and partnership approaches. The organisation is built on empowerment, and employees are highly valued within team-based or partnership relationships.

Seven skills or sensibilities of individual 'business athletes' are given as:

- ability to operate and get results without depending on hierarchical authority, position or status
- ability to compete in a way that enhances cooperation, and aims to achieve high standards rather than destroy competitors
- high ethical standards to support the trust which is crucial for cooperative approaches when competing in the corporate Olympics
- a dose of humility, with basic self-confidence tempered by the understanding that new things will always need to be learned
- process focus, with respect to the process of implementation as well as the substance of what is implemented
- multifaceted and ambidextrous approach to support cross-functional or cross-departmental work, alliances where appropriate, and the cutting of ties where necessary
- satisfaction in results, and willingness to be rewarded according to achievements.

The Challenge of Organizational Change: How Companies Experience It and Leaders Guide It

Co-authored with Barry A Stein and Todd D Jick, *The Challenge of Organizational Change* (1992) is a book on the management of change and is filled with practical examples. In line with many other writings on managing change, a distinction is drawn between evolutionary and revolutionary change, here described as 'long march' and 'bold stroke' approaches.

World Class: Thriving Locally in the Global Economy

World Class (1995) focuses on world-class companies with employees described as 'cosmopolitan' in type. These people are wealthy in terms of the 'three Cs' – concepts, competence and connections – and carry a more universal culture to all the places in which their company operates.

This knowledge-rich breed is set against 'locals', who are set in their ways, and the two groups are viewed as the main classes in modern society. The book is optimistic, in that Kanter believes stakeholders can influence world-class companies to spread best practices around the world.

Globalisation, it is argued, offers an opportunity to develop businesses and give new life to the regions. From her studies of regenerative areas, Kanter suggests that business and local-government leaders can work together to draw in the right sort of companies to create prosperity.

European as well as US successes are used to illustrate the benefits of globalisation, and the centrality of regional economies.

Rosabeth Moss Kanter on the Frontiers of Management

This book, published in 1997, brings Kanter's essays and research articles for *Harvard Business Review* together into one volume.

Evolve: Surviving in the Digital Culture of Tomorrow

In *Evolve* (2001), Kanter highlights the new networks of relationships that must evolve for people and organisations to succeed in the digital world. She introduces the idea of 'e-culture' and explores ways of adopting the principles of such a culture in an organisation. Her book contains many case study examples of companies that are succeeding or have failed in the digital world, and offers guidance on the skills managers need to accomplish the necessary change.

Confidence: How Winning Streaks and Losing Streaks Begin and End

Confidence (2004) explores the culture and dynamics of high-performance organisations, compared with those in decline, by explaining how confidence produces success in all types of situations. Drawing upon the experiences of sports teams, the perspective of the cycle of confidence is developed. This helps to explain why confidence grows in winning teams and helps propel a tradition of success, whereas in losing streaks it erodes and its absence makes it hard to stop losing. This thinking is applied to the business environment, and Kanter shows how confidence is the key to thinking big and bold rather than small and tentative.

A framework for turning confidence around is presented:

- The first stone – facing facts and reinforcing responsibility.
- The second stone – cultivating collaboration.
- The third stone – inspiring initiative and innovation.

Numerous sports and business examples are used to illustrate these ideas. Kanter concludes by exploring the role of leaders in building confidence and the personal life lessons for individuals.

Supercorp: How Vanguard Companies Create Innovation, Profits, Growth and Social Good

Research for *Supercorp* (2009) took three years. The book reveals that businesses that are succeeding are keeping ahead in terms of market changes and customer needs, and are also progressive, socially responsible human communities.

Numerous examples illustrate how companies are at the vanguard of linking business success and societal contribution. Vanguard companies are big but human, efficient but innovative, global but local.

Kanter looks at the opportunities created by this new business model and considers and explores the issues for strategy, business, people and society. She discusses a future agenda for managers and leaders.

In perspective

Kanter has the ability to present complex ideas in a way that many people to find accessible. Her books are well argued, well illustrated and supported by a wealth of practical research evidence. But above all they are readable and engaging. Some of her central ideas, once viewed by some as unrealistic, have now become absorbed into general management wisdom. These include change management, empowerment, participative management and employee involvement. Despite being over three decades old, her earlier works retain a freshness and relevance for today's business environment.

In *The Frontiers of Management*, she is presented as a groundbreaking explorer who has initiated a revolution in terms of new ways of working. It is also pointed out that some managers have still not crossed the frontiers, or do so in aspiration rather than actuality.

Her current areas of research include leadership for the digital age, looking at how and when leaders are empowered to create change; leadership of turnarounds; and multinationals and their impact on both the developed and developing world. Kanter chooses important economic and social issues to investigate and understand. She has always wanted to make an impact with her work and a significant contribution to improving the world.

Managing projects

Project management involves the co-ordination of resources to complete a project within planned time and resource constraints and to meet required standards of quality. It includes planning and allocation of resources and may make use of specialised management techniques for the planning and control of projects. Projects are usually considered successful if they meet predetermined targets, complete the intended task, or solve an identified problem without exceeding time, cost and quality constraints.

The project sponsor is the person responsible for the project and accountable to the business for its success. He or she chairs the project board.

The project board is the guiding or steering body that sets the standard for the project and makes the required resources available. It also monitors the delivery of the project outcomes. At each project milestone the project board also decides whether the project remains viable or whether the situation has changed and any redirection is needed.

The project manager is the person responsible for the day-to-day running of the project and leading the project team. He or she reports to the project board.

The management of a project is recognised as distinct from steady-state management or business as usual. Traditionally, the focus of project management has been the completion of defined tasks or activities within given time constraints and cost limits with a defined resource, and delivering final outputs to the customer at the required standard of quality. Today organisations of all kinds are increasingly relying on projects to implement business strategy and deliver desired outcomes. Managers are being asked to take on the management of specific projects and deliver project outcomes alongside their normal job responsibilities, and the ability to manage projects effectively has come to be seen as a key capability. Managers responsible for projects need to draw on a wide range of skills including planning, budgeting, team leading, delegation and people management. They must also be able to manage relationships with project team members and stakeholders.

A range of specialist methodologies and techniques are used in the delivery of projects, PRINCE2 (PRojects IN Controlled Environments) being perhaps the most widely known. This checklist, however, provides a generic framework for undertaking a project and offers a synthesis of current practice, incorporating elements from various approaches to project management. It outlines the major steps in the life cycle of a project and gives practical advice on the process of initiating, scheduling, executing and evaluating a project.

Action checklist

1 Define the objectives

Fundamental to the successful management of any project are a clear understanding of and agreement on certain factors by the project sponsor and the project manager.

These are:

- the aims and scope of the project
- the required outcome or result to be delivered
- dates and budgets for the completion of the project.

A lack of clearly stated project objectives and scope, agreed and understood by all stakeholders, will doom the project from the start. Time and resources may need to be allocated to this before making a final decision on whether the project should go ahead and will be a cost-effective means of achieving organisational aims.

2 Appoint the project manager

The project manager must be someone who has a proven track record, can command the respect of a mix of people at different levels in the organisation, and can motivate them to action and get results. The project manager should be able to:

- plan and communicate all aspects of the project
- create a work breakdown structure (WBS) that clearly identifies the constituent tasks of the project
- identify the resources required to deliver the desired outcome by creating an organisation breakdown structure (OBS)
- designate the right people for the right task at the right time
- motivate with integrity, sensitivity and imagination
- gain trust and enhance productivity through shared decision-making
- lead both by example and by taking a back seat when appropriate
- monitor costs, efficiency and quality without excessive bureaucracy
- get things done right first time without being a slave-driver
- use both technical and general management skills to control the project
- see clear-sightedly through tangled issues
- have the ability to recognise and resolve risks and potential difficulties.

3 Establish the terms of reference

The terms of reference for the project should specify the objectives, scope, time frames and initial scale of resources required and clearly identify project and payment milestones. They should also clarify any risks, constraints or assumptions already identified. It is important to make early allowances for cost escalation or plans veering off course, and to build in a level of contingency, such as a safety margin and control measures to minimise this risk. This information should be incorporated into a project initiation document.

4 Select and develop the project team

When assessing the resources needed to execute the project, personnel requirements should be at the forefront. If an existing team is to carry out the project, check whether they have the knowledge and skills needed. Is it necessary to second or appoint additional staff or to arrange training? If a new team is being brought together, you should make sure that you have the right mix of skills and experience. Consider also Meredith Belbin's work on the roles played by different team members.

Remember that it will take time for the members of a new team to develop good working relationships and start to perform at their best. The model of the stages of team development developed by educational psychologist Bruce W Tuckman may be helpful here. By monitoring how relationships are developing, keeping an eye out for potential problems and taking action to pre-empt or resolve conflicts, the project manager can create the right climate for the successful completion of the project. Responsibilities must be clearly allocated: this will avoid duplication of effort and reduce the potential for disputes over who does what.

5 Determine the activities needed to create the component elements of the project

Having established what the project should achieve and drawn up a WBS, consider how to execute the work. Activities should be sequenced so that they can be integrated into the final output of the project. The resources needed to achieve each element of the work should be identified, as this will assist in drawing up schedules, taking into account the inevitable resource constraints. The resulting schedule or Gantt chart then becomes the basis for implementation.

6 Plan for quality

By planning for quality early in the project, major risks, costs and reputational damage can be avoided later in the project's life cycle. Planning for quality requires both paying attention to detail and ensuring that the project output or outcome does what it is supposed to, or is fit for purpose. Planning for and assuring quality at every stage helps ensure that the final output from the project is of a suitable quality standard. Quality measures (systematic inspections against established standards) should be built into the process from the beginning, not later when things (may) have started to go wrong. Use the formula below:

Establish standards > Monitor performance > Take corrective action

This can run as a continuous sequence throughout the project. The key is to ensure effective quality assurance which acts preventatively rather than as a cure and enables you to get things right first time.

7 Estimate costs

This is crucial, as the most frequent error in project management is the underestimation of costs. Typical cost elements include:

- staff time and wages – usually the most substantial cost item of all

- overheads – employer on-costs

- materials and supplies – the raw materials

- equipment – the pros and cons of leasing or purchasing and the depreciation factor

- administration – purchasing, accounting, record-keeping.

  Among the enabling functions of good budgeting are the monitoring of costs while a project is in progress, and the setting of appropriate levels of contingency as described in point 3 above.

8 Set the project schedule

To calculate the shortest time (critical path) necessary to complete the project, you need to know:

- the earliest time a stage or unit can start
- the duration of each stage
- the latest time by which a stage must be completed.

  Gantt charts, programme evaluation and review techniques (PERT) and critical path analysis (CPA) are popular project management techniques that can help with the effective prioritising and scheduling of activities.

9 Monitor and report progress to stakeholders

Monitoring of in-progress costs, timescales and quality is essential and should be carried out constantly throughout the project. Quality is the hardest area to measure and, as such, is often at risk of neglect. The key point about monitoring progress is that reports must be accurate, timely and provide the right sort of management information to keep the project sponsor and other stakeholders fully informed. This will ensure that important decisions can be made when necessary.

The management of threats can have a strong bearing on the success of a project. Early identification of risks and problems can provide a basis for mitigation and, where required, for contingency planning, and can help to ensure the delivery of successful projects.

10 Deliver the output

Steps preceding the delivery of the project outcome may include the compilation of instructional documentation or training packages. The penultimate stage before project completion is ensuring that the outcome of the project is acceptable to the customer or sponsor. You should consider whether the report or other outputs will be understood by and acceptable to the intended audience, such as senior managers within the organisation who will have to sign off the project or agree to implement its recommendations.

11 Evaluate the project

By building in a final stage of evaluation it is possible to gain a measure of the project's success and see what lessons can be learned; ideally there should be evaluations after each major phase of a project. Once again, the three key areas for review are quality, time and costs. Others include:

- staff skills gained or identified
- mistakes not to be repeated
- tools and techniques that were valuable
- what should be tackled differently next time.

Organisations can benefit by developing a central resource containing project evaluations and lessons learned, although these documents need to be open and candid about failures as well as successes if they are to be useful to the managers of future projects.

As a manager you should avoid:

- taking too little time to clarify objectives, terms of reference and delivery schedule
- forgetting to build in quality checks
- failing to monitor and report on progress to all stakeholders

- allowing the project to exceed time and budgetary limits
- neglecting to monitor small changes and assess the possible implications
- allowing 'project creep', whereby the scope of the project is allowed to expand without a clear decision-making process.

Participating in projects

A project is a carefully selected set of activities chosen to use resources (such as time, money, energy, space, provisions) to meet predefined objectives and to support business goals, usually with agreed start and end dates. In contrast to business as usual, projects are unique, one-off activities. Projects are a common feature of the modern workplace, and in many organisations several projects will be in progress at the same time. Multiple projects may be grouped together in a portfolio or programme designed to deliver strategic benefits to an organisation.

For an employee, participating in projects can broaden experience, provide exposure to other parts of the business, and develop skills in teamworking, communication, influencing others, change management, risk management, project planning and project control. Participation in projects can be stimulating, motivational and developmental. It may ultimately lead to career progression. For an employer, encouraging participation in projects has the advantage that it draws on employees' critical skills and knowledge (at whatever level in the organisation) and can make their work more interesting. Projects can foster cross-functional understanding and teamworking and drive efficient and effective collaboration across the organisation.

At the same time, if, as an individual, you are asked to participate in a project, you need to weigh up the advantages against a number of other factors. Will the project have a destructive effect on your ability to do your day-to-day job? Do you have the skills to participate in the project and contribute effectively? Is the project, or your participation in it, fraught with complications and internal politics that will ultimately be damaging to your reputation or your chances of career progression? Projects are a common vehicle for development and can be hugely beneficial to your personal development and career, but it is wise to consider the bigger picture before getting involved.

This checklist looks at how managers can be involved in projects and keep up with their regular job responsibilities. It is aimed mainly at managers with little experience of participating in projects, but it may be helpful for more experienced managers as well. Project managers may also find this checklist a useful tool for understanding the perspective of other members of their project team.

Action checklist

1 Understand project prioritisation within organisations

At the organisational level, projects need to be prioritised in some way. An organisation has limited resources and has to ensure that these are devoted to activities that will maximise the return on investment. It is unlikely that all project ideas or activities can be pursued, so it is good practice to filter these through an evaluative process. One approach is to set up a project proposal and business case template that must be completed for all new project proposals. This document can then be submitted for approval so that resources can be allocated appropriately. Proposals can then be evaluated together regularly at senior management or board level, perhaps monthly, quarterly, biannually or annually, depending on the size of the organisation.

2 Be clear about your responsibilities

Find out precisely what the project leader will expect of you and consider whether you will be able to meet the requirements. Overload can lead to stress, inefficiency, errors and loss of enthusiasm and motivation, so if necessary be prepared to say no to the project, rather than take it on and fail with the project and/or your regular work responsibilities. Assess the politics of the project. What are the underlying reasons for your involvement? Are there any hidden risks if you are unable to deliver on any aspects of the project that you have responsibility for?

It is also important to make sure you have the right skills to fulfil the responsibilities allocated to you. Beware of being handed a task that appears to be a great opportunity but is in fact risky and tricky, and could well backfire on you if the project is unsuccessful. Assess any offers or requests carefully and seek advice from a trusted colleague or friend if in doubt. If you do not have a choice in the matter, make clear any reservations you have at the outset.

Document your understanding of the project requirements and agreements, then send copies to both your boss and the project leader. Be prepared to negotiate on these with both parties and adjust them accordingly. The final document should give you a clear, agreed mandate, even though things will change as the project progresses. It also means that the scope of your involvement and your areas of accountability are documented. This will help to prevent 'project creep' and will make the extent of your responsibilities clear if anything goes wrong at a future date.

Nevertheless, if you are happy with the responsibilities involved, make the most of the different opportunities available to you in the project team

3 Balance work priorities

Review your priorities carefully. Discuss the implications with your boss and the project leader, preferably together. Consider:

- how much time you will need to give to the project and when
- where you will have to be to carry out the project requirements
- how these requirements will affect your regular activities
- what should happen when (not if) there is a conflict of priorities

- what should happen when (not if) the situation changes
- what additional resources you may be able to call on, if necessary
- whether any regular activities could be postponed or normal standards allowed to slip
- how frequently the situation will need to be reviewed.

4 **Make adjustments and manage your time**

Everyone has limited time and energy, so you will need to try to find a way of prioritising project work and other tasks. Discuss with your manager how you might adjust routine work or manage time more effectively. For example:

- delegate some regular responsibilities to someone who might be glad of the development opportunity
- adjust work schedules to give you more disposable time for the project's duration
- be realistic rather than perfectionist – aim for good enough where appropriate
- encourage effective project meetings with timed agendas, team status reports and action point minutes
- do not attend meetings when you have no contribution to make and will see the minutes afterwards
- do not try to read all paperwork in detail – instead, scan all but short or important items
- handle immediate actions quickly, and plan the time to handle the rest
- allocate your toughest items to your most productive time of day
- discourage constant interruptions – instead, set interruptible and uninterruptible periods.

At times, you will just have to do the best you can to cope with extra workloads, but do not let this get out of hand. When priorities clash, discuss the conflict and how to resolve it with your boss and your project leader.

5 Manage project relationships

A project has many players, including the project sponsor, project leader and project team members. There may also be an intermediate programme manager, if there are a number of linked projects. Remember your relationships will go beyond the immediate project team – there will be assorted stakeholders who will contribute or are affected by the project in some way.

The principal project management relationships are those with the project sponsor, who is accountable for success and has to own the project, and the project manager, who is responsible for delivery on behalf of the sponsor and must be given the necessary authority by the sponsor to exercise his or her responsibilities effectively.

The responsibilities of the project sponsor are to:

- draft and agree the business case
- determine the prioritisation of a project and set success criteria
- select and approve the project manager
- gain resources for and commit them to the project (e.g. people, money, space, equipment)
- approve the project leader's projected estimates of cost, schedule and scope of work
- handle key stakeholders and suppliers
- assess the project manager's performance
- oversee risk management
- approve core team members and provide assistance in securing them
- shield the team from politics and non-value-added outside influences
- be aware of and report on the project's status
- maintain support for and commitment to the project leader and team.

The responsibilities of the project manager are to:

- negotiate with the project sponsor (and programme manager, if appropriate) regarding the initial scope of work, schedule duration and resource needs
- write the project management plan
- act as the main focal point for the project
- secure the commitment of team members
- communicate the project goals and requirements to all team members
- address customer needs throughout the project
- lead the team through the planning process
- run the risk management process
- run the stakeholder management process
- manage change
- track project progress and initiate any corrective action to keep the project to plan
- communicate the project's status to the project sponsor, team members and interested customers
- raise potential issues or current problems where necessary
- support the project team.

The responsibilities of project team members are to:

- be directed by the project leader, and maintain an enthusiastic, positive and proactive attitude
- be involved in planning the project, and contributing requirements and information from their department and customers
- be involved in setting the project team's ground rules and adhering to these
- contribute positive, creative suggestions at team meetings, but understand that these may not always be acted on
- support team decisions

- assist and support other team members
- accept responsibility and take ownership for their own activities and decisions
- track their own activities and stay on schedule
- keep the project leader informed
- be involved in the risk assessment
- inform the project leader at an early stage of any risks, overspends or project delays.

6 Reap the benefits

The main benefits of being involved in projects alongside regular work activities are as much yours as your organisation's. But you do need to take advantage of these, deliberately and consciously. Projects can be tremendous learning experiences, so do consolidate learning by reflecting regularly on the new knowledge and skills you have acquired and consider how you can continue to apply what you have learned in day-to-day activities. Use a CPD (continuing professional development) scheme to record your activities, learning and reflections.

You will also benefit from:

- ensuring that your boss and project leader know what you have achieved by providing regular, brief status reports
- sharing your knowledge by coaching others – this will be beneficial to you as well as to them
- enhancing your visibility by letting others know what the project has achieved, for example by giving briefings or presentations at departmental meetings
- volunteering for other projects.

As a manager you should avoid:

- agreeing to anything that is impossible – projects can be a poisoned chalice in some cases, so make sure you are not chosen as the scapegoat

- pushing yourself or others too far, even if you feel energised and excited
- getting so involved that you neglect your regular work responsibilities
- trying to hide problems relating to either the project or your regular activities.

Henry Laurence Gantt
The Gantt chart

Introduction

Henry Laurence Gantt (1861–1919) left a popular legacy to management: the Gantt chart. Accepted as a commonplace project management tool today, it was an innovation of worldwide importance in the 1920s. But the chart was not Gantt's only legacy; he was also a forerunner of the human relations school of management and an early spokesman on the social responsibility of business.

Life and career

Gantt was born into a family of prosperous farmers in Maryland in 1861. His early years, however, were marked by some deprivation as the civil war brought about changes to the family fortunes. He graduated from Johns Hopkins College in 1880 and was a teacher before becoming a draughtsman in 1884 and qualifying as a mechanical engineer. From 1887 to 1893 he worked at the Midvale Steel Company in Philadelphia, where he became assistant to the chief engineer (Fredrick W Taylor) and then superintendent of the casting department.

Gantt and Taylor worked well in their early years together, and Gantt followed Taylor to Simonds Rolling Company and on to Bethlehem Steel. From 1900 Gantt became well known in his own right as a successful consultant, as he developed interests in broader, even conflicting, aspects of management. In 1917 he accepted a government commission to contribute to the war effort at the Frankford Arsenal and the Emergency Fleet Corporation.

Gantt's contribution

Gantt is often seen as a disciple of Taylor and a promoter of the scientific school of management. In his early career, under the influence of Taylor and with his own aptitude for problem solving, Gantt attempted to address the technical problems of scientific management. Like Taylor, Gantt believed that only the application of scientific analysis to every aspect of work could produce industrial efficiency, and that improvements in management came from eliminating chance and accidents. Gantt made four individual and notable contributions.

1 The task and bonus system

Gantt's task and bonus wage system was introduced in 1901 as a variation on Taylor's differential piece-rate system. With Gantt's system, employees received a bonus in addition to their regular day rate if they accomplished the task for the day, and they still received the day rate even if the task was not completed. By contrast, Taylor's piece-rate system penalised employees for substandard performance. As a result of introducing Gantt's system, which enabled workers to earn a living while learning to increase their efficiency, production often more than doubled. This convinced Gantt that concern for the worker and employee morale was one of the most important factors in management, and led him eventually to part company with Taylor on the fundamentals of scientific management.

2 The perspective of the worker

Gantt realised that his system offered little incentive to do more than just meet the standard. He subsequently modified it to pay according to time allowed, plus a percentage of that time if the task was completed in that time or less. Hence a worker could receive three hours' pay for doing a two-hour job in two hours or less. But here Gantt brought in an innovation: paying the foreman a bonus if all the workers met the required standard. This constituted one of the earliest recorded attempts to reward the foreman for teaching workers to improve the way they worked. In *Work, Wages and Profits* (1910), Gantt wrote:

Whatever we do must be in accord with human nature. We cannot drive people; we must direct their development … the general policy of the past has been to drive; but the era of force must give way to that of knowledge, and the policy of the future will be to teach and lead, to the advantage of all concerned.

Gantt was interested in an aspect of industrial education which he called the 'habits of industry' – habits of industriousness and cooperation, doing work to the best of one's ability and pride in the quality as well as the quantity of work.

From his experience as a teacher, Gantt hoped that his bonus system would help to convert the foreman from an overseer and driver of workers to a helper and teacher of subordinates.

3 The chart

Gantt's bar chart started as a humble but effective mechanism for recording the progress of workers towards the task standard. A daily record was kept for each worker: in black if they met the standard; in red if they did not. This expanded into further charts on quantity of work per machine, quantity of work per worker, cost control and other subjects.

It was while grappling with the problem of tracking the various tasks and activities of government departments on the war effort in 1917 that Gantt realised he should be scheduling on the basis of time rather than quantity. His solution was a chart that showed how work was scheduled over time through to its completion. This enabled management to see, in graphic form, how well work was progressing, and indicated when and where action would be necessary to keep on time.

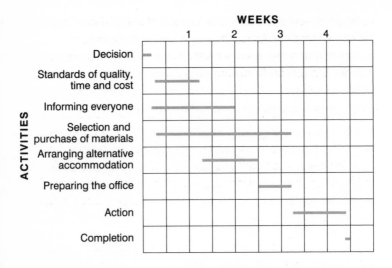

Figure 1: Gantt chart – redecorating an office

Gantt charts have been applied to all kinds of projects to illustrate how scheduling may be best achieved. Figure 1 shows a Gantt chart for a mini-project of redecorating an office. The steps are:

- establishing the terms of reference and standards of quality, cost and time
- informing all appropriate personnel and customers
- arranging alternative accommodation
- preparing the office
- redecorating.

The Gantt chart provided a graphic means of planning and controlling work and led to the development of PERT (programme evaluation and review technique) diagrams.

4 The social responsibility of business

After the death of Taylor in 1915, Gantt distanced himself further from the core principles of scientific management and extended his management interests to the function of leadership and the role of the firm itself. As his thinking developed, he believed increasingly that management had obligations to the community at large, and that profitable organisations had a duty towards the welfare of society.

In *Organizing for Work* (1919), he argued that there was a conflict between profits and service, and that a businessman who says that profits are more important than the service he renders 'has forgotten that his business system had a foundation in service, and as far as the community is concerned has no reason for existence except the service it can render'. These concerns led him to assert:

The business system must accept its social responsibility and devote itself primarily to service, or the community will ultimately make the attempt to take it over in order to operate it in its own interest.

Gantt was hugely influenced by events in Russia in 1917, and, fearing that big business was sacrificing service to profit, he began to attack the profit system itself, calling for public-service corporations to ensure service to the community.

In perspective

Gantt's contributions to the advancement of management science are of great significance. He was a prolific writer and speaker, addressing the American Society of Mechanical Engineers on a number of occasions. Several commentators have noted that one of his papers, *Training Workmen in Habits of Industry and Cooperation* (1908), gives a unique insight into the human relations dimension of management at a time when scientific management was at its peak.

His approach to the foreman as teacher marks him as an early contributor to human behavioural thought in a line that stretches back to Robert Owen, forward to Elton Mayo and up to the present day. His approach to the duty of the organisation towards society also singles him out as one of the earliest spokesmen on the social responsibility of business. But it is as the inventor of the Gantt chart that he will be remembered.

It has been suggested that his thinking became somewhat vague shortly before his death, as he began to set the work of the organisation in a broader national and political context. It seems that there was a struggle in his later years between service and appropriate rewards on the one hand and socialist control policies on the other.

Gantt never profited from his enduring innovation, and his books are illustrated with examples of charts showing work in progress rather than the lateral project bar chart with which we are more familiar today. He received a Distinguished Service Medal from the government, but it was a member of Gantt's consulting firm, Wallace Clark, who first coined the term Gantt chart in 1952 and popularised the idea of the chart in a book that was translated into eight languages.

Feasibility studies

A feasibility study is an initial investigation into a proposed project or initiative (such as a product, activity, new business or change programme) to estimate whether it is likely to be successful and/ or profitable, if carried out. The building blocks of a feasibility study may vary according to context, but they should include estimates of the resources required (materials, time, personnel and finance) and the expected return on investment.

Feasibility studies are typically used in project management, but they are also carried out in many other areas, especially where new investment is concerned. These include proposed business ideas, organisation or strategy changes, new products or business improvements.

There are differing views about the value of feasibility studies. Critics suggest that they are of little use except as a tool for obtaining funding, pointing to the fact that projects often go ahead despite less than promising results from the feasibility studies. They can also be expensive and time-consuming to carry out. Others would argue, however, that feasibility studies can be invaluable in identifying problems, mistakes or false assumptions within a proposal, or helping to work out which approach to a new initiative gives the best chance of success.

The contents of a feasibility study depend to some extent on the context and the reasons for undertaking it. A study examining a proposed solution to a previously identified problem, for example, will differ in content from one relating to an innovation initiative or the exploitation of a new opportunity. In general, the study will examine the proposal and gather sufficient information to assess whether the project or initiative is suitable for the organisation and fits with its strategy and direction; whether the organisation has the resources and capabilities required to carry it out; and whether it is likely to succeed in terms of meeting the desired objectives or making a profit.

In some cases, external consultants are engaged to carry out feasibility studies. This can give organisations the benefit of experience and expertise that is not available in-house. If the decision is to use a consultant, it is important to manage the process carefully. This checklist assumes that a feasibility study is being carried out in-house and provides a basic format for managers to follow. It also provides an insight into the process of conducting a study for those using consultants.

Action checklist

1 Name your feasibility study

A feasibility study may be undertaken to evaluate a variety of proposals, from suggested changes in approach or organisation to ideas for a new project, product, activity or business. Throughout this checklist the subject of the feasibility study will, for the sake of brevity, be referred to as the proposal or the idea. It is helpful to start by considering how to name the study so as to make its objective clear. Be as precise as possible, giving readers an immediate understanding of what the study and the identified problem or need will address.

2 Summarise your plan

After establishing an appropriate name for the study, compose a brief opening summary of your proposal and the problems or opportunities the study addresses. Add any other supporting details you think necessary.

3 Identify benefits and other opportunities

Summarise the benefits or opportunities that you expect will be gained for clients or the organisation from your proposals. To some extent, the information-gathering, research and analysis stages of the study will enable you to add to these later on.

Be clear from the start that whoever reads the study and evaluates the proposals will have little time to spare. This means that your objective must be to gain the reader's attention from the first page, and hold it through a combination of attractive propositions and easily understood text. Summarise your data, research or analysis throughout the main text, and include the full details for reference at the end.

4 Gather supporting information

You are likely to have gathered a good deal of information while developing your idea, but you now need to identify exactly what is needed to evaluate your proposal in detail, both to supplement what you already have and to consider potential problems or alternatives. This process will continue as you work your way through subsequent stages of the feasibility study. At the start, however, you may find it helpful to carry out internet and literature searches to pick up on sources that you may have missed previously. These might be relevant reports, periodicals or more current data.

Provide general background information on the organisational or market context that supports a need for the action or changes you are proposing, remembering that concision and clarity are all-important. These will relate to the nature of the proposals but could include, for example, demographic, environmental, social, economic, political, legal and technological trends and developments.

5 Stakeholder analysis

Stakeholders include all internal or external departments, teams, organisations or individuals involved in, or affected by, the implementation of your idea. Stakeholder groups are likely to include clients or customers, senior management, suppliers, colleagues, operational teams affected, regulatory bodies, government agencies, and/or the local community. You should establish which groups are involved, what their needs and expectations are, how acceptable the proposals are likely to be to them, and how they might be encouraged to contribute to the success of your idea. Questionnaires, interviews or focus groups might be used to explore the views and objections of the various groups involved, and will also help to engage them by gaining their interest and, hopefully, their support. Consider whether different groups of stakeholders will be affected in positive or negative ways, and try to address the concerns of those that may oppose the idea.

6 Evaluate constraints and alternative options

First, identify internal or external restrictions that could limit or block the achievement of your objectives. For example, internal constraints could result from technological, time or cost barriers. Restricting policies or long-term strategies might also be a limitation – for example, a corporate decision to outsource an area would block ideas favouring internally initiated innovations or solutions to the problem.

Second, consider whether there are preferable options that might achieve the same results as the approach you are proposing in the feasibility study. Evaluate these in terms of time, cost or resource implications, simplicity and staffing.

To explore and establish the value of your approach compared with others, you might, for example, focus on exceeding customer needs, challenging some current assumptions, reframing some current views, emphasising quality rather than just the cheapest options, and drawing upon stakeholders' views. Techniques that could help to make the analysis more reliable include decision tree analysis, Monte Carlo simulation, sensitivity analysis and scenario analysis.

7 Research the opportunity

Market analysis and resource analysis are both crucial if you want to establish the feasibility of a new business, product or service. Although in-depth research is not usually required at this stage, enough information is needed to give a good idea of your market and the competitive environment, and should therefore include the following:

- likely levels of demand, sales expectations
- target markets for new businesses, products or services
- market and organisational benefits of potential changes or improvements
- the expected availability of resources for meeting the proposed objective(s).

The nature of the project or idea studied will dictate the areas for analysis. For example, for a property development such as converting industrial buildings into homes, factors to consider could include the availability of similar local accommodation, numbers of vacant properties, potential competitors and their development plans, the possibilities for growth in demand, level of income generation, and the likely time periods for leases or rentals.

Longer-term projects or research may require a first feasibility study to define and map out the main areas that will later become the subject of further feasibility studies of multiple or staged areas of the project.

8 Research the costs and cost the benefits

The costs and benefits that may result from your proposals are key to establishing their financial feasibility. Cost comparisons between various approaches, resources, materials, overheads and suppliers could be basic to your research, covering such items as:

- capital goods – for example, buildings or equipment

- overheads/operating costs – costs for people, transport, raw materials, production and/or operation

- support services – possible agency or service charges you need to cover

- sources of finance and interest costs – sources of, and likely costs of interest on, financing to fund your proposals.

  The costs will then be set against the expected returns or other benefits you define and are likely to include the following:

- **Revenue projections.** These projections link to any sales estimates or customer benefits you define, and may come directly from your market research.

- **Benefit analysis.** Benefits should be measurable where possible, so try to think of ways of establishing evidence of the positive results that will be derived from any softer, less tangible benefits. For example, while it can be argued that better customer service will increase revenues, hard figures are usually required by those considering investing in your proposals. You could, therefore, suggest or carry out a comparative pilot study to explore its actual effects.

9 Assess the risks

All proposals and plans involve a degree of uncertainty, which is a basic element of planning for the future. Although a detailed risk analysis is unlikely to be appropriate at the feasibility stage, it will be helpful to consider what sort of risks might be involved. To do this, identify:

- possible sources of risk

- effects that could be expected

- responses that could be made to deal with them

- how risks might be prevented, mitigated or managed.

10 Set an approximate timetable

Time is money, and an approximate timetable is necessary at the feasibility stage to help those responsible for final decisions to put the resource implications of your study (such as finance, equipment, staffing, and admin) into a timescaled context.

As a manager you should avoid:

- seeing an unsuccessful feasibility study as a failure – it has functioned successfully if it has identified in broad terms the potential benefits and the obstacles and risks the project may attract

- treating a feasibility study as a business plan – a good feasibility study may provide information for a business plan, but its main aim is to identify risks and problems.

Developing a business case for a new product or service

A business case is a structured document used for presenting a project proposal. The case justifies the implementation of a product or service within the organisation, and details the costs involved in executing and maintaining the initiative. Most importantly, it highlights the anticipated business benefits offered by its introduction.

The introduction of new initiatives is crucial if organisations are to enhance business performance and evolve in an ever-changing business market. Typically, an organisation will have to make a choice between several business ideas, only a small proportion of which it will be able to fund in any one financial year.

Suggestions for introducing a new product, service or practice, or indeed amending existing ones, are detailed within a business case. Business cases are used for project investments in a wide range of sectors and industries and for a number of different reasons.

The business case provides the evidence needed to support the proposal, justifying the initial investment of staff time, funds and resources required to carry out the initiative, measured against the projected long-term business benefits. By highlighting the reasons for undertaking the scheme, senior management can gauge the most profitable business investment ideas by comparing each proposal and assessing its value.

Action checklist

1 Composition of the business case

The business case will usually be presented in two different ways: a written document followed by an oral presentation. The composition of the written business case will typically include the following:

- **Introduction** – the purpose of the proposal and the reasons for undertaking the project.

- **Business objectives** – how the project will meet wider organisational objectives and fit in with existing strategy.

- **Options considered and recommended solutions** – pros and cons of alternative scenarios and/or products.

- **Project scope** – the parameters of the project.

- **Assumptions** – this could include factors such as estimates of the economic life of the product, usage, development schedule, etc.

- **Costing, benefits and financial implications** – see point 2 below.

- **Investment appraisal** – a comparison of the costs of developing, operating and maintaining the project measured against the benefits and savings expected from its introduction.

- **Proposed timescale** – the length of time required to implement the initiative. The business case will, on average, cover three to five years.

- **Risk and mitigation** – the possible risks of implementing the project with counterbalancing solutions.

- **Communications strategy** – how communication with key players will be maintained throughout the project's life cycle.

- **Achievability** – is the organisation able to deliver the new product or service at present? Do new systems or infrastructure need to be invested in to make the product or service viable?

This list is by no means exhaustive, but it includes the characteristic elements of a standard business case. Additional information could also include details of the end user, success criteria, project sponsor, technical requirements, and roles and responsibilities of key players. Before deciding which elements to include in the business case, you need to ascertain whether your organisation has an existing format for project proposals. If so, adhere to it. It is also essential to find out if there are any criteria against which the business case will be judged and, if so, what these are.

2 Cover costing, benefits and financial implications

Your project is likely to be competing with others to gain approval. Therefore senior managers will be examining its practicality and value, and assessing whether it is a profitable way of spending the organisation's budget. To give your proposal the best chance of being accepted, you must show that the return on investment justifies the initial outlay required to put the idea into action. Your proposal will be scrutinised by many different parties, so make sure your evidence is watertight. The case should be made either in added value terms (i.e. the income generated will exceed the cost of implementation) or on the basis of the return on investment (i.e. the cost of the investment is justified by the financial returns it offers). Additional financial elements to consider in your proposal are as follows:

- **Business benefits and savings** – an estimate of the monetary value of the benefits and savings to be gained. Make an estimate based upon the knowledge you have of the anticipated users of the product or service. Where possible, state the benefits and savings in measurable terms, avoiding adjectives such as better, cheaper, or faster.

- **Project cost** – a calculation of the development costs of the proposed idea and the time frame over which these costs are accrued.

- **Operational cost** – a calculation per year of the costs of operation and maintenance, for example operational staff, equipment use, raw materials.

- **Discounted cash flow** – inflation will affect the value of a product over time. Therefore, if you propose to introduce a product, you will need to apply a discount factor to calculate its value in, for example, five years' time.

3 Emphasise the benefits

Focus on the business benefits of your proposal rather than the costs involved in its implementation and maintenance. In particular, stress the financial benefits so that stakeholders can see a correlation between these and the cost of launching the scheme. Emphasise the foreseen advantages for both the wider organisation and for the individuals to whom the case is being presented.

Although benefits such as customer satisfaction, saving staff time and resources, gaining a competitive advantage, enhancing business reputation and innovation will enhance your proposal, they are nevertheless difficult to measure. Therefore your audience may prefer hard financial facts and accurate projections. Nevertheless, provision of non-financial measures such as key performance indicators (KPIs) and anticipated benefits can also add value to the proposal, particularly if these provide a way of measuring success post-implementation. Do try, where you can, to provide solid evidence to give your case the best chance of acceptance

4 Provide supporting evidence

To present your proposal as a viable and realistic investment, show that you have made realistic projections of the return on investment and have taken into account all the costs involved in its execution. Estimate future income using supporting evidence such as a like-for-like comparison, or the results of a pilot scheme that shows the innovation has already worked well within the organisation and represents good practice. Put details of this evidence in your appendices. Do not hide any risks or disadvantages inherent in your case. Simply present alternative courses of action that can be undertaken to counterbalance any problem areas. Demonstrate that you have taken account of the inherent risks involved in your project as well as its advantages.

5 Gain support

Gaining senior management support is crucial for the success of your proposal. Such backing is necessary for obtaining the funding and resources required. The importance of this cannot be underestimated; if key stakeholders do not feel included or involved in shaping the proposal, you may not be able to rely on their support later on.

It can often be worth trying to get the support of individual senior managers in advance of presenting the final business case. This allows any objections or concerns they may have to be addressed in advance and an assessment to be made of how likely your proposal is to succeed. Whether this approach can be adopted will depend on organisational practice and culture. However, once you have gained the initial interest of senior management, you will need to present your case to key stakeholders and those who will carry it out.

6 Present the case

Once you have written and circulated the business case, the next stage in selling your idea is to make an oral presentation of your proposal to stakeholders and other interested parties. To convince others to invest in your project, you must demonstrate that you believe wholeheartedly in your endeavour and its success. Consider how best to present your case to optimise its impact. The audience and the culture of the organisation will largely determine the way you do this. Depending upon the content of the case, it can be handled in several ways:

- If it is a complicated proposal, accompanying literature may act as a guide, but do not just print out handouts of your presentation.

- If PowerPoint presentations are used, make them effective. Use them to back up your points, rather than explain the words you are saying in detail.

- Visual aids, such as a flip chart, can help to accentuate key elements, but be careful not to use them too heavily or they may lose their impact.

  Your audience's attention must be captured from the outset. Begin by outlining your proposal, its benefits and costs, and communicate how the case will be developed. The case should be concise and well argued, taking no more than five minutes to present. You should not assume that your audience have read your original report, so do not refer to it repeatedly. An effective summary brings together all the key points of your proposal in a concise manner, so a sound closing speech is essential. You should also make it plain what input you require from others in order to execute your project, so that your audience is left in no doubt as to the level of involvement needed.

7 Rehearse your case

As with any endeavour, practice makes perfect. Time yourself, analyse your proposal and try to see it from your audience's perspective. What objections might be raised? Are there any evident gaps in your business case? As with an interview scenario, try to anticipate possible questions you may be asked, typically what, why, how, who and when, such as:

- What will it cost?

- Why should current practice be changed?

- How is the change to be made?

- Who will be involved in its implementation?

- When should it be completed?

  Your case needs to be polished, professional and to the point. Most importantly, make sure that you have checked all the facts that support your project, especially the financial projections.

Consider committing key figures to memory so that questions can quickly be answered without referring to documentation.

8 Understand your audience

To make certain that the presentation is pitched at the right level and is communicated successfully using appropriate language, you first need to gain an understanding of who your audience are. Your audience's support is critical for success, so try to anticipate their reaction as far as possible.

9 Deal with objections

Although thorough preparation will reduce the number of objections, it will not eliminate them entirely. Sensitive issues such as risk, cost, resources and time will inevitably invite challenge. And different members of your audience will have different objectives depending upon the position they hold within the organisation. So be prepared to be questioned and challenged on various facets of your business case.

10 Respond to objections

One method of dealing with objections is to offer alternative scenarios. For example, if there is an objection to one aspect of the proposal, suggest another viewpoint so that the benefits of your proposal are highlighted from a different angle. Offering choice puts your audience in a position of control, as it provides them with the authority to make a decision. Providing several different options for your audience to consider also gives them something to deliberate, thus reducing the possibility of them instantly dismissing your idea out of hand. However, you still need to be clear why you made your initial recommendations; state your case with confidence, and answer every objection with a benefit.

11 Maintain communication

Once your project has been approved, it is important to monitor and communicate its progress to interested parties regularly. Develop a communications strategy to achieve this objective. Keep track of the proposed timescales presented in the business case to ensure that the project does not run over time. The business case should be used to keep the project on track, so maintain momentum by continually reviewing the progress and status of the project.

As a manager you should avoid:

- presenting costs and benefits without substantiating evidence
- underestimating or hiding implementation and operational costs
- presenting the business case without first rehearsing and analysing its content
- failing to understand your audience
- losing project momentum once the proposal has been accepted.

Richard Tanner Pascale
Change, agility and complexity

Introduction

Richard Tanner Pascale (b. 1938) came to prominence in the early 1980s, when Tom Peters and Robert Waterman's *In Search of Excellence*, published in 1982, was aiming to redefine the route to corporate success. Pascale's *Art of Japanese Management* (co-authored with Anthony Athos and published in 1981), expounding the virtues of the McKinsey 7S model, has become a classic and he has remained at the forefront of management thinking ever since. Pascale is also known for his work on organisational agility and the Honda effect, complexity in organisations and, more recently, positive deviance. He is a successful business consultant, author and academic.

Life and career

Pascale gained an MBA from Harvard Business School and was a Baker Scholar. In the late 1970s, while he was a consultant at McKinsey, he was heavily involved in the evolution of the 7S model developed by Peters and Waterman. He was a member of faculty at Stanford's Graduate School of Business for 20 years and taught organisational survival, which became the school's most popular course, as part of the MBA. He is now an associate fellow at Saïd Business School, University of Oxford.

Pascale has acted as an adviser to the White House and as a consultant to many *Fortune* 500 companies, from AT&T to Shell.

During 2005, he was adviser to the US ambassador in Iraq, being in control of the transition of the new ambassador into his post and the management of the largest US mission in the world.

A critic of fads, Pascale, like many of his contemporaries, does not want to be known as a guru or expert. Such labels, he believes, bring about a mindset of 'hero with all the answers', and he would rather be recognised as someone who keeps addressing questions as they occur and recur. To that end, Pascale spends a number of days each year focusing on questioning and learning from discussions with business leaders.

Key theories

Japanese management and the 7Ss

A spirit of inquiry brought Pascale and Athos into contact with Peters and Waterman in the late 1970s, when Waterman was driving a McKinsey initiative to seek out new models of corporate success. Peters and Waterman went on to cite US examples of success in their 1981 bestseller, while Pascale and Athos looked at lessons from Japan and how they were being applied in corporate America. What brought the four of them together was the accelerating pace of business change and the increasing inadequacy of corporate information systems that had been sufficient in the past. Both *In Search of Excellence* and *The Art of Japanese Management* expounded the 7S theory, but it was Pascale and Athos who explored it in greatest depth, tracing many of its origins to working practices in Japanese organisations, particularly Matsushita Electric Company.

Comparing Matsushita with ITT, Pascale and Athos found that the two organisations were differentiated more by softer elements of management style, staffing policies, skills and shared values than by their systems, structure or strategy. In the early 1980s, the 7Ss – usually presented in the shape of a circle or diamond – were as original for their juxtaposition of concepts not previously considered important as for their communicability through alliteration. The 7Ss comprise three hard factors:

- Strategy – how the organisation gets from where it is to where it wants to be.
- Structure – how the firm is organised.
- Systems – how information moves around.

And four soft factors:

- Style – patterns of behaviour of senior management.
- Staff – not just numbers, but the characteristics of those who live and work at the organic centre of the organisation.
- Skills – distinctive capabilities of individuals or of the organisation as a whole.
- Superordinate goals (shared values) – not so much bottom-line targets as meanings and values that are pervasive throughout the organisation and knit together individual and organisational purposes.

Ambiguity and uncertainty

In *The Art of Japanese Management* Pascale and Athos describe how managers are increasingly faced with situations that are neither clear nor susceptible to resolution by the application of rational analysis. These situations arise out of the conflicts, ambiguities and uncertainties that stem from the four soft Ss: style, staff, skills and shared values. Rather than forcing a final solution, the authors suggest, it may be better to accept the lack of clarity in the situation, and simply decide to proceed. Proceeding should yield further information, and the best course may be to move towards the goal by a sequence of tentative steps rather than by bold, striking actions.

Organisational agility and the Honda effect

Pascale's 1984 article, 'Perspectives on Strategy: the real story behind Honda's success', juxtaposed two contrasting views on the rise of Honda in the US: the Boston Consulting Group's account of Honda's success, and Honda executives' own explanation of it. The article stimulated much debate over the role and value of corporate strategy in business decision-making, summarised in a 1996 article, 'The Honda effect revisited', by Henry Mintzberg and others.

BCG attributed Honda's success to long-term investment in technology and economies of scale instead of short-term profitability. Pascale did not aggressively dispute this, but found it did not explain why the then still-young Honda had embarked on an apparently reckless US strategy in the first place. Interviewing a number of Honda executives, Pascale became aware that the story was characterised more by miscalculation, chance and learning-on-the-spot than by the logical, analytical progression that emerges from BCG's rational account.

Pascale explained the Honda effect as a Western preference for the oversimplification of reality, and for linear explanations of events that overlook the process through which organisations experiment, adapt and learn. This preference leads to a failure to appreciate that an organisation's way of dealing with miscalculations, mistakes and chance events that are outside its defined plan is often crucial to its success over time.

The key to Honda's success, concluded Pascale, was organisational agility. He continually returns to this theme, believing it to be a core organisational competence.

Pascale's five conclusions summarising the Honda debate propose that:

1 Organisational agility is increasingly important as a source of renewable competitive advantage.

2 Agility resides in what an organisation is rather than what it does. In *The Art of Japanese Management*, Pascale cites Harold Geneen's attempt, while chief executive of ITT, to reduce uncertainty through quantification and controls. Matsushita, however, he pictures as a Pied Piper, more in tune with the uncertainty and imperfection that exists in all organisations, and

operating on a basis of shared values and beliefs created by a philosophy linking work to social as well as productive ends.

3 The interaction of four key dimensions makes an organisation what it is:

- Power – can employees really influence the course of events?

- Identity – do individuals identify with the organisation as a whole?

- Contention – how is conflict brought out into the open and used creatively?

- Learning – how does the organisation handle and develop new ideas?

  Within Honda, for example, employees are empowered to take pioneering action and share an enterprise-wide identity in cross-functional teams. Debate, experimentation and inquiring attitudes are actively encouraged.

4 Strategic intent and agility depend upon the norms, values and behaviours communicated within the social system of the organisation. Pascale refers to Honda's efforts to institutionalise responsiveness, adaptability and external focus.

5 Agility depends on certain organisational disciplines, such as continuing dissatisfaction with the status quo; managing back from the future; uncompromising straight talk and bringing differences out into the open; and harnessing adversity by learning from setbacks and adapting to move forward.

Complexity, chaos and letting go

In a 1999 article, 'Surfing the Edge of Chaos', Pascale addresses what he considers to be the biggest challenge facing organisations today: how to increase the number of workable and winning strategic initiatives. He builds on the principles of the science of complexity:

- a complex adaptive system is at risk when it is interfered with and controlled – equilibrium precedes extinction

- complex adaptive systems are capable of self-organisation and of generating new methods of operating

- some complex adaptive systems can move towards the brink of chaos before new patterns emerge and new forms of organisation take shape

- complex adaptive systems cannot be directed or strictly controlled.

In drawing parallels between the world of complex scientific systems and the world of organisations, Pascale tests these four principles against a period of change at Shell, through interviews with Steve Miller, the director driving Shell's renewal initiative. Pascale concludes the article by quoting Miller's words – that is, not by summarising and generalising, but by going into the depth and individuality of the organisational context itself. It is interesting to look at some of Miller's comments (paraphrased below) and relate them to the above four principles:

- You have to recognise that the top can't possibly have all the answers.

- The actual solutions about how to best meet the challenges of the moment, those thousands of strategic challenges … have to be made by the people closest to the action.

- The leader becomes a context setter.

- Once the grassroots realise they own the problem, they also discover that they can help create and own the answers.

- There's another kind of risk to the leaders … the risk of exposure. Before, you were remote from them, now, you're very accessible.

- Finally, the scariest part is letting go … you get more feedback than before … you know more through your own people about what's going on in the marketplace … but you still have to let go of the old sense of control.

Positive deviance

This new approach to problem solving and improving performance is presented in Pascale's book *The Power of Positive Deviance* (2010), co-authored with Jerry and Monique

Sternin. The key to positive deviance, say the authors, is to learn from your own organisation's experiences. Look for examples of individual learning breakthroughs, of individuals succeeding against all expectations. Understand their practices and replicate and disseminate them throughout the organisation or wider community.

The positive deviance process must be owned by the employees, not management – give responsibility to the employees. Be aware that this process can be time-consuming. The authors use first-hand experiences of real-world problems, such as malnutrition in Vietnam, staphylococcus infections in hospitals and infant mortality, to illustrate how the positive deviance process can help.

In perspective

Pascale's research, consulting and exploration continue to lead him to redefine what makes organisations tick. Although he does not fit easily into any predefined category of management theorist, he remains both at the front and at the edge in seeking new ways of understanding organisations. Pascale has sought to explore the processes of change by trying to understand their complexities and interdependencies, not by reducing his findings to mechanistic formulas. In line with his own advice to organisations, he himself exhibits a lack of complacency in his efforts to understand the right pieces, before fitting them into the organisational jigsaw.

He describes his work on complexity as a 'big idea', and, although it builds on established principles of complexity theory, it will no doubt seem a little strange at first, particularly to those who want to eradicate uncertainty.

Conducting a risk assessment for projects

A risk assessment establishes the various threats that could compromise a project and, should they arise, analyses the impact they will have upon the project's success. Each risk is ranked in relation to the severity of the effect, ranging from a low-level risk to a high-level threat.

Completing projects on time and within budget can be a significant challenge for project managers. Problems can often be caused by the unforeseen problems or risks that transpire throughout the project. Project managers cannot predict every unforeseen problem, but they can take a proactive step towards spotting potential risks by undertaking a risk assessment.

Risk assessments can help project managers effectively determine the likelihood of a risk occurring, and, should it arise, assess the impact it is likely to have on the project's success. Risks can arise at varying degrees of severity, having a detrimental effect upon the project's cost, timescale and performance. However, unforeseen events can also lead to opportunities as well as threats. Early detection means that appropriate strategies can be formulated in advance and implemented if required, minimising the impact of threats and maximising the potential benefits of opportunities.

Carrying out a thorough risk assessment at the project's initiation stage, and monitoring the threats throughout the project, assures the project manager that in the event of the worst-case scenario happening, the project's success will not be severely compromised.

Action checklist

1 Identify project risks

Draw up a preliminary list of potential risks by holding a brainstorming session with key members of the project team. This group should consist of the senior members of the project team, together with a variety of personnel at different organisational levels. It is also beneficial to invite those representing the customer and/or the supplier (if applicable) for an additional perspective. This diverse mix will offer varying viewpoints and assist in the generation of ideas.

The size and scale of the project will affect the length of these sessions and the number of people participating. However, it is recommended that six to fifteen people attend, with the session ideally lasting between one and two hours. Additional time can always be allocated at a later date if further ideas need to be considered. The average number of risks identified from the session can be anything from twenty to sixty. Make sure that ideas are written down, perhaps on a flip chart, so that they can be reviewed, ordered and placed into categories after the meeting. Ensure that all risks are understood before the end of the meeting to enable accurate ranking and categorising.

2 Rank each risk

Once the initial list has been drawn up, the next step is to rank each risk. An attempt should be made to reach a consensus among the group. The risks are scored against two criteria:

- the probability of occurrence– typically following a nine-point scale, where one is the lowest (least likely to happen) and nine is the highest (most likely to happen)

- the severity of impact on the project if the risk occurs.

These two variables are considered in relation to the project time frame, cost and performance. Mark each risk using a simple scoring band such as high, medium or low:

- high – will have a serious impact on the project time frame and cost as well as seriously affecting related projects

- medium – will have an impact on the project with possible consequences for any related projects, with some effect on the costs but a serious effect on the timescale

- low – will have a less significant impact on the project in terms of schedule and little effect on costs.

The probability of occurrence and impact can be detailed on a grid such as a risk-ranking matrix. Use such a tool to identify the top ten greatest risks to ensure that they receive the merited level of attention. Once each risk has been scored, this information is then recorded in the risk register.

3 Composition of a risk register

A typical risk register includes three different types of fields: descriptor, risk category and management.

Descriptor fields

These include:

- **Title** – a concise and clear description of the risk.

- **Description** – details of the precise issues involved with the risk. The description should also contain the process that is being undertaken for risk mitigation.

- **Likelihood** – the chance of the risk occurring. The use of banding (high, medium and low) is one method of measuring this field.

- **Impact** – this can also be categorised into high, medium or low bands. The impact will be a grouping of severity in terms of cost, time and performance.

- **Cost** – this can be presented as an actual price or as a percentage. For example, a high risk could be a 65% increase in the budget or a £1 million single payment.

- **Time** – this is the delay in the project schedule if the risk arises. It can be difficult to measure the exact time frame of a delay, so if in doubt, overestimate to ensure that the risk is given due attention.

Risk category fields

Incorporating category fields within your risk register is a helpful means of ordering your identified threats and is especially recommended if you have twenty or more different risks. Such category types may include resources, environmental, technical, operations, and so on. Categorising will also help you to discern any obvious trends, which in turn will help you to devise strategies to mitigate them. ⟩ Trends -

Management fields

These include:

- **Nominee** – the person most suited to monitoring and managing the risk who will take responsibility for the ownership of the risk. Recording the nominee enables the register to be used for auditing purposes.

- **The bearer** – the person who bears the consequences if the risk occurs.

- **The source** – this field is used to determine whose fault the risk is, for example a supplier or a third party.

4 Update the risk register

It is necessary to consult and review each threat frequently regardless of its impact level. A low risk may suddenly gain medium or high-risk status as the project develops, and vice versa. As well as monitoring existing risks, new threats may be identified as the project develops. Any changes must be recorded so that the register remains an effective project management tool. Key project stakeholders should be informed of any significant changes to risk ranking and ordering, as this may affect the project schedule, performance and cost.

5 Mitigate the risks

Ranking and recording risks in the register will help you devise contingency plans for reducing and controlling potential threats. Your response to controlling the risks and making them more manageable should be documented in the risk register. There are five courses of action to choose from. You can pick one or a combination of the following:

- **Transfer** – assigning risk responsibility to someone who is better suited to managing it. This may be a third party, such as an insurance company.

- **Eliminate/prevent** – counterbalancing measures that either prevent the risk from arising, or stop it from affecting the project if it does occur.

- **Mitigate** – actions that decrease the chances of risk occurrence, or reduce impact to a manageable level.

- **Contingency** – planned actions that are implemented as and when the risk occurs.

- **Acceptance** – in some cases it may be inevitable that the risk will arise and mitigation is not possible. This is when the contingency plan comes into play.

Reducing and controlling project threats will help to ensure your project is delivered successfully on time and within budget.

6 Produce a risk model

A risk model can be used to produce a set of consistent results that will enable you to make a valuable risk assessment based upon reliable evidence. It should be constructed to include all the identified project risks and the factors affecting their manageability. The model needs to be a realistic representation of the risks and should reflect the unknown elements of the project. Modelling software can be used to model project risks to obtain a set of reliable results.

Apply varying ranges of measurable values such as time and

cost to each risk to give you the full scope of possible outcomes. Ranges should be in actual terms (e.g. time, cost) as well as in percentages. Run the simulation software repeatedly for all the different ranges and record the summary results after each rerun. To ensure consistency of results, run the program again, but this time change the starting point for the algorithm (which produces the numbers at random). Compare the results of the two different starting points. Repeat the simulation until the result is steady and thus reliable.

7 Produce the risk management plan

The risk management plan informs the wider project team of the extent to which you will be managing the identified risks, and details how you intend to achieve this. It should set out a number of tasks that each team member is responsible for undertaking in order to manage their assigned risks.

Before you begin the allocation process, consult the register to identify the most urgent risks requiring immediate attention. Once this is ascertained, develop a plan of action for curtailing or mitigating each risk. As well as focusing on the top ten most urgent risks, action plans should also be drawn up in readiness for those risks with a score of six or over. The action plan should include:

- the designated team member responsible for carrying out the action
- completion timescale
- instances when the owner(s) should communicate with the project manager for additional decisions
- the resources required to fulfil the action.

The action plan must be drawn up immediately, whereas the mitigation plan is drawn up periodically to reduce low-level risks. There is no set recommended length for the plan, but do bear in mind that colleagues are unlikely to have the time to read a lengthy document, so every effort should be made to be as concise as possible.

8 Produce the risk assessment report

Once the data from the risk register and the risk model have been collected and collated, a realistic cost and time frame for the project should become clear, and you should have gained a sound understanding of the aspects of the project that could go wrong and why. The next step is to produce a report, communicating your findings to those responsible for the project and addressing the implications of the results. The report should clearly demonstrate the level of risk to the project, emphasising any urgent action required. The cost implications for putting your proposed contingency plans in place need to be clearly spelled out.

As a manager you should avoid:

- failing to update the risk register regularly
- underestimating the level of risk to the project's success by ranking risks too low
- failing to revisit all the identified risks throughout the project
- identifying and ranking risks without input from the whole project team
- running the risk model simulation too few times and thus failing to gain consistent and reliable results
- ignoring initially low-level risks that may acquire high-level status as the project matures
- attempting to mitigate every risk – some risks may be unavoidable
- failing to recognise that some unexpected eventualities can provide fresh opportunities
- incurring significant overhead costs where low-probability, low-impact risks are concerned.

Total quality: mapping a TQM strategy

Total quality management (TQM) is a style of managing that gives everyone in the organisation responsibility for delivering quality to the end customer, quality being described as 'fitness for purpose' or 'delighting the customer'. TQM views each task in the organisation as fundamentally a process that is in a customer/supplier relationship with the next process. The aim at each stage is to define, meet or exceed the customer's requirements in order to maximise the satisfaction of the final consumer at the lowest cost.

TQM efforts typically draw heavily on previously developed tools and techniques of quality control. TQM enjoyed widespread attention and popularity during the late 1980s and early 1990s before, in its turn, being overshadowed by newer approaches to managing quality. These include ISO 9000, a set of international standards for running a business in an effective manner; lean management techniques, which focus on eliminating waste in operational processes that fail to create value for the customer; and Six Sigma, which seeks to improve the quality of process outputs by identifying and removing defects and their causes.

The introduction of a TQM strategy is a major strategic decision requiring considerable research and planning, and it is important to combine the hard edge of quality (its tools and techniques) with the soft side of cultural change. The successful implementation of TQM should lead to improvements in the quality of products and services, reductions in the waste of resources, and overall increases in efficiency and productivity. These improvements contribute to good customer relations, growth in market share and sustained competitive advantage. TQM involves the whole organisation and needs to become a way of life if it is to be successful. This checklist focuses on the process of planning for the introduction of TQM in an organisation.

Action checklist

1 Establish a planning team

You will need a team of suitable people to drive through the changes associated with TQM. In a small organisation this will be the senior management team; in a larger one it should include senior managers representing the major functions or departments. Include known sceptics or critics in the team and ensure that minority views are represented. Many organisations have found that a cross-functional, multi-level team provides the best mixture of views, perspectives and ideas.

2 Assess the need for change

Consider the competitive position of the organisation. Establish who your main customers are and find out what they expect; do not assume that you are currently meeting all their requirements. Bear in mind that discovering what customers need is a continuous rather than a one-off process. Establish how relevant groups – suppliers, competitors and employees – view the quality of your products and/or services.

3 Define the vision

Draw up a vision statement defining where the organisation wants to be in terms of serving its customers; this vision must be stretching but attainable. Define the principles and values that underpin the vision. Use other organisations as a model but make sure the statement reflects your own culture and circumstances. The statement must ensure that TQM supports the organisation's long-term vision and is aligned with broader organisational strategy and objectives.

4 Define the standard of service you aim to provide

Translate the vision into realistic and measurable outcomes. Define what customers, suppliers and employees expect the organisation to deliver in terms of quality of each product and/or service.

5 Review how you are currently performing against standards

You may discover a large gap between customer expectations and reality. Establish the reasons for this across the organisation. Common causes of poor quality include external constraints, being let down by suppliers and internal inefficiencies. It can also be the case that customers expect too little, so it is important to assess their needs as well as their expressed wishes.

6 Conduct an assessment of current levels of waste

Quantify the quality failures by obtaining an assessment of current levels of waste from heads of departments. Ensure that all employees are involved in the assessment. Collect data as widely as possible, produce costings and present the findings to the senior management team.

7 Establish the current cost of waste

Work out how much is currently spent on rectifying internal failure (for example, reworking or replacing poor-quality goods) and external failure (for example, handling customer complaints). Include appraisal costs: the time and money spent on inspection and checking.

8 Decide whether to go for third-party certification

You need to decide whether to seek accreditation for your quality initiative, for example a third-party certification scheme such as BS EN ISO 9000. This can help to gain recognition from customers and suppliers and in some cases may even be demanded by them. This should not be treated as an extra project, but as a confirmation of the existing good practices that have already been documented.

9 Draw up your quality strategy

Use the results of the waste audit to draw up your quality strategy, covering:

- the goals of the strategy, including a revised statement of your mission, if necessary
- the systems and tools needed to change processes
- the cultural changes needed to create the right environment for quality
- details of the resources that can be applied
- the time frames.

Secure senior management approval for the plan.

10 Draw up an action plan for change

Translate your strategy into detailed plans for action. Bear in mind that organisational culture will be a critical factor in the success or failure of the initiative. Strong and effective teams are essential, so plan for the introduction or strengthening of team-based working if appropriate.

11 Establish an education and training programme

Some staff will need in-depth training, others will need less, but everyone should be given a thorough introduction to TQM and made aware of what it means for them in their work role. Carry out an analysis of training needs in relation to TQM and cost the additional training required. This can be offset against the expected productivity gains. Plan for:

- general induction and training of all employees in the principles of TQM

- development of managers, supervisors and team leaders in the soft skills needed to implement TQM
- job-specific training in new techniques associated with TQM
- additional training in customer relations.

An external trainer or facilitator is almost always essential, especially in the early stages, unless internal expertise is available.

12 Set priorities for improvement

Set priorities for the introduction of TQM. Select key processes for early analysis and improvement. Do not try to cover everything at once; start with no more than three processes. Choose at least one that is likely to demonstrate quick returns in business performance.

13 Goals and criteria for success

You will need to set both short-term and long-term targets and establish measures of success in both business and cultural terms.

As a manager you should avoid:

- going ahead without full support from senior management
- seeing TQM as a quick fix
- introducing TQM at the same time as other new initiatives
- using TQM (or even appearing to use TQM) as a means of downsizing.

Total quality: getting TQM to work

The successful implementation of TQM can lead to improvements in the quality of products and services, reductions in the waste of resources, and overall increases in efficiency and productivity. Such improvements contribute to good customer relations, growth in market share and sustained competitive advantage. To be effective, however, TQM needs to be implemented consistently across the organisation. Implementation should evolve into a process of continuous improvement that becomes a way of life for everyone in the organisation.

TQM is not a single process, but rather a philosophy and commitment to continuously striving for better quality. There are many different approaches to TQM and no universal way in which it can be defined and measured, but there are a number of organisations across the world that certify comprehensive approaches to TQM and offer accreditation to organisations implementing it. Many of these approaches focus on self-improvement efforts across the organisation, designed to increase efficiency and customer satisfaction. In its early days, TQM was very much the province of manufacturing and process businesses. However, the principles of TQM can be applied at least as well in service and non-profit organisations.

This checklist focuses on the implementation process and assumes that a TQM strategy has already been developed.

Action checklist

1 Consider running pilots

It is important to map a TQM strategy to cover the whole organisation, but it is usually best to introduce it in stages. For pilot stages, select areas or functions which are significant and where you feel TQM can yield results quickly – within a year at most. This will be critical to gaining evidence of TQM's benefits and support for broader implementation across the organisation.

2 Monitor and evaluate the results of the pilots

Draw up a framework and appoint a management team to assess and evaluate the results of the TQM pilots. Identify lessons to be learned, and consider how best to apply these when introducing TQM elsewhere in the organisation.

3 Decide which tools and techniques to use at each stage

Four key stages in the implementation of TQM are measurement, process management, problem solving and corrective action. For each of these, select tools and techniques that are appropriate to the scale and environment of your organisation.

4 Decide which measurement techniques to use

Measurement is critical. It enables situations and events to be successful, ensures that TQM activity is always dealing with an accurate view of a process, outcome or problem, and provides benchmarks to use when evaluating progress. It is crucial to ensure that measurement is a meaningful process that leads to corrective and improvement action, not just an end in itself. Some of the main techniques that can be used include measurement and error-logging charts, corrective action systems, work process flow charts, run charts and process control charts.

5 Select process management tools

A range of systems and tools are available for process management, some of which are probably already used in your organisation. These include Gantt charts, flow charts, histograms and others. Select the approaches that fit best within your organisation's culture.

6 Set up mechanisms for problem solving

Plan to establish a range of groups throughout the organisation to look at improving quality from different perspectives:

- **Improvement groups** are regular sessions for work teams, led by supervisors.

- **Key process groups** analyse the operation of important processes.

- **Innovation groups** are cross-departmental, cross-level groups that focus on potential, and totally new, ways of working.

Techniques these groups can use include brainstorming, fishbone diagrams and Pareto analysis.

7 Set up corrective action mechanisms

The emphasis in TQM must be on discovering the causes of less than optimal performance, identifying problems and solving them. At the planning stage, build in feedback loops that will highlight problems so that corrective actions can be taken.

8 Plan to create the right culture for quality

Successful TQM depends as much on cultural change as on process improvements. TQM can be effective in breaking down barriers between different functions and departments or silos so that new ways of thinking can lead to better ways of doing things together. Be aware that a general programme of information and education targeted at employees, supervisors and managers will needed.

9 Draw up a communications plan

Decide when and how to announce the TQM programme across the organisation. Assume that some staff may be sceptical, and work out strategies for overcoming this. Use pilot-stage converts, if possible, to explain the benefits of TQM, and explain how the TQM initiative relates to others that may be running in the organisation.

10 Implement an education and training programme

As part of your TQM strategy, implement your education and training programme. Target key groups first, and use change agents to cascade what they have learned throughout the organisation.

11 Empower supervisors

Team leaders are pivotal to TQM success. You need to give them the resources, time, support and education they need to become good, inspiring leaders.

12 Motivate employees to take ownership

TQM depends upon employees taking ownership of quality and acting on their own initiative. As change-oriented thinking becomes a habit for all employees, the value TQM can add to business processes and operations will become clear, with a positive impact on the bottom line. To achieve this, you will need to create an open culture and drive out fears of failure, blame or risk taking. It may also be necessary to manage the potential insecurities of people who discover that some of their work is unnecessary, or can be carried out by less qualified staff.

13 Establish a programme of management change

In a traditional organisation, profound changes in management style will be needed. Employees will not be able to make the required changes without a fresh approach, based on collaboration, consensus and participation. The largest single change for managers will be the shift in management and communication style, from commanding to empowering, from telling to listening.

14 Set short- and long-term goals for the implementation programme

Establish a means of monitoring progress. This will require a mix of short-term goals to demonstrate progress and more challenging, longer-term goals that will stretch the organisation. Include a mix of hard business and soft cultural indicators.

15 Maintain the impetus

Cultural changes take a long time to produce visible results. Be patient, and keep people's enthusiasm and engagement alive through constant communication. Review and report on progress regularly. Encourage the publication of project successes throughout the organisation, and strive to make all participants champions of the programme.

16 Keep track of and share the results

It is crucial to keep everyone informed on progress, impact and benefits, in order to maintain and reinforce commitment. It is important to share things that do not work as well as successes, so as to provide learning opportunities and drive further improvements.

As a manager you should avoid:

- treating TQM as a precisely defined methodology or sequence of steps
- thinking of TQM as a quick fix rather than a process of continuous improvement
- trying to implement TQM at the same time as other major change initiatives

- losing sight of TQM's ends by concentrating too much on the means
- expecting instant results
- equating TQM with quality control.

Glossary of terms associated with TQM

Corrective action – depends on introducing management systems that require employees to identify the cause of a problem and remove it permanently.

Fishbone charts or cause-and-effect diagrams – explore the root causes of a problem in diagrammatic form.

Gantt charts – used in planning projects to show the proposed start and finish of each activity graphically, against a common timetable.

Histograms – bar charts that show patterns of variation in different processes.

Pareto analysis – used to separate out and prioritise significant items in a mass of data by applying the 80/20 rule. Recording and analysis often show that 80% of problems stem from 20% of potential causes.

Process control or process flow charts – used to plot the sequence of events for a particular process in a sequential diagram.

W Edwards Deming
Total quality management

Introduction

William Edwards Deming (1900–93) is widely acknowledged as
the leading management thinker in the field of quality. He was
a statistician and business consultant whose methods helped
hasten Japan's recovery after the Second World War and beyond.
He developed the first philosophy and method that allowed
individuals and organisations to plan and continually improve
themselves, their relationships, processes, products and services.
His philosophy is one of cooperation and continual improvement;
it avoids blame and redefines mistakes as opportunities for
improvement.

Life and career

Born in Iowa in 1900, Deming's modest upbringing in an early
settler community was to instil habits of thriftiness and a dislike
of waste which were to influence his later thinking. His academic
career started at the University of Wyoming, where he achieved
an engineering degree in 1921, followed by a master's degree
in mathematics and physics from the University of Colorado.
He completed his studies at Yale University in 1928, where he
was awarded a doctorate in mathematical physics. Deming then
concentrated on lecturing and writing in mathematics, physics
and statistics for the next ten years.

In the late 1920s Deming became familiar with the work of

Walter Shewhart, who was experimenting with the application of statistical techniques to manufacturing processes. Deming became interested in applying Shewhart's techniques to non-manufacturing processes, particularly clerical, administrative and management activities. After joining the US Census Bureau in 1939, he applied statistical process control to their techniques, which contributed to a sixfold improvement in productivity. Around this time, Deming started to run courses for engineers and designers on his – and Shewhart's – evolving methods of statistical process control. At Stanford University, Deming taught the Stanford statistical training programme to nearly 2,000 people in a couple of years, using the Shewhart cycle for learning and improvement and the PDCA (plan–do–check–act) cycle.

Deming's expertise as a statistician was instrumental in his posting to Japan after the Second World War as an adviser to the Japanese Census. At this time, the US was the leading economic power, with products much envied by the rest of the world; it saw no need for Deming's new ideas. The Japanese, however, recognised that their own goods were shoddy by international standards. Moreover, after the war, they could not afford the wastage of raw materials resulting from post-production inspection processes and were consequently looking for techniques to help them address these problems. While in Japan, Deming became involved with the Union of Japanese Scientists and Engineers (UJSE), and his career lecturing to the Japanese on statistical methods and company-wide quality, a combination of techniques now known as total quality management (TQM), began.

It was only in the late 1970s that the US became aware of his achievements in Japan. In the 1980s there was a spate of publications explaining his work and influence. In his American seminars during 1980, Deming talked of the need for the total transformation of the Western style of management. In 1986 he published *Out of the Crisis*, which documented the thinking and practice that had led to the transformation of Japanese manufacturing industry. Just before he died in 1993 he founded the W Edwards Deming Institute.

Summary

Deming's work and writing constitute not so much a technique as a philosophy of management, total quality management, that focuses on quality and continuous improvement but which has had – justifiably – a much wider influence.

Deming's interest in variation and his approach to systematic problem solving led to his development of the fourteen points, which have gained widespread recognition and are central to the quality movement and his philosophy of transformational management. Deming's seven deadly diseases of management and his use and promotion of the PDCA cycle, known to many as the Deming wheel, are described below.

Variation and problem solving

The key to Deming's ideas on quality lies in his recognition of the importance of variation. In *Out of the Crisis*, he states:

The central problem in management and in leadership … is failure to understand the information in variation.

Deming was preoccupied with why things do not behave as predicted. All systems (be they the equipment, the process or the people) have variation, but he argued that it is essential for managers to be able to distinguish between special and common causes of variation. He developed a theory of variation: that special causes of variation are usually easily attributable to quickly recognisable factors such as changes of procedure, change of shift or operator, etc, but that common causes will remain when special causes have been eliminated (normally because of design, process or system). These common causes are often recognised by workers, but only managers have the authority to change them to avoid repeated occurrence of the problem. Deming estimated that management was responsible for more than 85% of the causes of variation. This formed his central message to the Japanese.

Fourteen points for management

Deming created fourteen points that provide a framework to developing knowledge in the workplace and guide long-term business plans and aims. They constitute not so much an action plan as a philosophical code for management. They have been extensively interpreted by many commentators on quality.

The fourteen points apply to any organisation, large or small, from service companies to manufacturers. They are as follows:

- Create constancy of purpose towards improvement of product and service, with the aim of becoming competitive, staying in business and providing jobs.

- Adopt the new philosophy. Western management must awaken to the challenge, must learn their responsibilities and take on leadership for change.

- Cease dependence on mass inspection. Build quality into the product from the start.

- End the practice of awarding business on the basis of price tag alone. Instead, minimise total cost. Move towards a single supplier for any item, based on a long-term relationship of loyalty and trust.

- Improve constantly and forever the system of production and service to improve quality and reduce waste.

- Institute training and retraining.

- Institute leadership. The aim of supervision should be to lead and help people to do a better job.

- Drive out fear so that everyone may work effectively for the company.

- Break down barriers between departments. People in research, design, sales and production must work as a team, to foresee and solve problems of production.

- Eliminate slogans, exhortations and targets for the workforce, as they do not necessarily achieve their aims.

- Eliminate numerical quotas in order to take account of quality and methods, rather than just numbers.
- Remove barriers to pride of workmanship.
- Institute a vigorous programme of education and retraining for both the management and the workforce.
- Take action to accomplish the transformation. Management and workforce must work together.

Seven deadly diseases of management

Deming described the main barriers faced by management to improving effectiveness and continual improvement – he was referring to US industry and its management practices:

- Lack of constancy of purpose to plan products and services that will have a market and keep the company afloat.
- An emphasis on short-term profits and short-term thinking (just the opposite from constancy of purpose to stay in business), fed by fear of unfriendly takeover, and by demand from bankers and owners for dividends.
- Evaluation of performance and annual reviews.
- Mobility of managers and job-hopping.
- Management by use only of available data.
- High medical costs.
- High costs of liability.

Deming said that effective management and a commitment to quality were needed to combat these seven deadly diseases. He emphasised the importance of communicating quality messages to all staff and building a belief in total quality management.

The relevance of these principles to a wider general management application has contributed to Deming's status as a founder of the quality management movement, not just quality and process control. This is why he interests an audience that is much wider than the quality lobby.

PDCA cycle (the Deming wheel)

Walter Shewhart originated the concept of the PDCA (plan–do–check–act) cycle and introduced it to Deming. Deming promoted the idea widely in the 1950s and it became known as the Deming wheel, also the Deming cycle.

The cycle consists of four steps or stages that must be gone through to get from problem faced to problem solved. Repetition of these steps forms a cycle of continual improvement:

- Plan for changes to bring about improvement.
- Do changes on a small scale first to trial them.
- Check to see if changes are working and to investigate selected processes.
- Act to get the greatest benefit from change.

In perspective

Naturally, no one as universally acclaimed as Deming can escape without criticism. Some have criticised his approach as being good for improvement but uninspiring for creativity and innovation. Some say his approach is not effective for generating new products or penetrating new markets. Others, particularly Joseph Juran, another quality guru, think there is an overreliance on statistical methods. Deming's US lectures in the 1980s, however, point time and time again to a mistaken preoccupation with the wrong type of statistics. He argued against figures focusing purely on productivity and control, and argued for more evidence of quality, a message that Tom Peters adopted in the 1980s and 1990s.

Deming stirred up wide interest with his denial of management by objectives and performance appraisals. Similarly, his attitude towards integrating the workforce has led TQM to be perceived as a caring philosophy. Paradoxically, his focus on cost reduction has been pointed to as a cause of downsizing.

Although in the 1980s the US paid tribute to Deming – not only for what he did in Japan, but also for his thinking and approach to quality management – few US companies used his methods. One reason for this may be that by the 1980s Deming was selling a system that worked, that he implied that he had discovered the only way to achieve quality, and that he was no longer alert to changes in the problems. In Japan, in the beginning, he had listened to Japanese needs and requirements, showed them respect and developed his thinking with them. In the US in the early 1980s, he appeared to try to dispense his philosophy rather than adapt it to a different culture.

In 1951, in early recognition of their debt to Deming, the UJSE awarded the Deming Prize to Japanese organisations excelling in company-wide quality. It was not until the late 1980s that the US recognised Deming's achievements in Japan and elevated him rapidly to guru status. The 1990s showed that Deming's legacy is likely to have a lasting and significant impact on management theory. Why is this?

The first reason must be the nature of his achievement. Deming has been universally acclaimed as one of the founding fathers of TQM – if not the founding father. The revolution in Japanese manufacturing management that led to the economic miracle of the 1970s and 1980s has been attributed largely to Deming.

Second, if the fourteen points make less of an impact today than they did just after the Second World War in Japan, it is probably because many aspects of them have now been adopted, assimilated and integrated into management practice, and they have been continuously debated and taught in business schools around the world.

The third reason is more complex, and lies in the scope of his legacy. Deming's fourteen points add up to a code of management philosophy which spans the two major schools of management thought that have dominated since the early 20th century: scientific (hard) management on the one hand, and human relations (soft) management on the other. Deming succeeds – despite criticisms of overuse of statistical techniques

– in marrying them together. Over half of his fourteen points focus on people as opposed to systems. Many management thinkers veer towards one school or the other. Deming, like Peter Drucker, melds them together.

Deming's approach was fresh and original. His philosophy came not from the world of management but from the world of mathematics; and he wedded it with a human relations approach that came not from management theory but from observation, from seeing what people needed from their working environment so as to contribute of their best.

Implementing business process re-engineering

A process can be defined as a series of linked activities that transform one or more inputs into one or more outputs. Re-engineering is a means of initiating and controlling change processes through imaginative analysis and systematic planning.

In their book *Re-engineering the Corporation* (1993), Michael Hammer and James Champy defined business process re-engineering (BPR) as:

The fundamental rethinking and radical design of business processes to achieve dramatic improvements in critical contemporary measures of performance, such as cost, quality, service and speed.

BPR gained widespread popularity during the 1990s following the publication of the book, which introduced a radical new approach to organising activities and operations across an organisation designed to streamline processes, improve efficiency and reduce costs.

Although many successes have been driven by BPR, critics of the technique have drawn attention to cases where companies failed to achieve the expected results. Reasons put forward for the failure of re-engineering projects include a tendency to confuse the introduction of more efficient processes with downsizing; too great an emphasis on reducing staff numbers; poor redesign of processes; the retention of a departmental focus, as opposed to a process-driven, customer-focused culture; the introduction of new technology without due attention to operational needs; and, most critically, a failure to involve staff at every stage.

There is a growing realisation that the human element should be at the forefront of BPR projects, as this is often the most challenging aspect of any change programme. It has also become clear that BPR techniques are valuable, not just in introducing high-level organisational change, but in re-examining minor functions. Indeed, it is often at the lower levels that significant rewards can be reaped. Successful re-engineering requires a clear understanding that:

- organisations should be process-driven not function-driven
- processes must be built around the customer
- staff involvement at all stages of design, planning, implementation and maintenance is a prerequisite for success.

Hammer has stated that process re-engineering on its own is not enough to improve organisational performance. BPR needs to be complemented by a range of additional changes (to performance measures and pay systems, for example) that encourage a focus on corporate, rather than departmental objectives. It is essential to put customers at the centre of all processes; to share responsibility and empower employees; and to move away from confrontation towards the building of collaborative partnerships with suppliers and even, when appropriate, with competitors.

Improvements in process quality to be gained from BPR have three dimensions:

- process efficiency (e.g. cost, cycle time)
- product quality (e.g. customer satisfaction, scope and quality of product)
- reduced product development time.

This checklist provides a guide to the key stages in implementing business process re-engineering.

Action checklist

1 Develop the vision

Start by making sure that any re-engineering efforts will support the organisation's mission, vision and objectives. You need to be clear about the answers to questions such as: What business are we in? What is our current position? Where do we want to be in, say, five years? How do we aim to get there? Who and where are our customers? Do we have a clear customer-focused vision?

It is important to create a bold, clear vision for BPR, but one that is rooted in reality. Draw up an outline strategy with ambitious but achievable goals for the organisation which will gain the support of senior management.

Be clear about the scope of the BPR project. Is this a major organisation-wide initiative or will it focus on specific lower-level processes that need attention? Identify key business processes and critical success factors for business performance, and plot them on a matrix to show priorities for action and help you decide where to deploy resources to achieve the maximum improvements in the short term. Survey techniques can be applied to assess customer opinion, benchmark the competition and analyse existing skills and competences across the organisation. Identify gaps between what is currently available and what will be needed in terms of skills, investment, IT and other resources.

2 Map existing processes

Take into account the degree of change required: is it radical change or a re-examination of minor activities? Map and document current processes and workflows to an appropriate level of detail, depending on the scope of the project. Endeavour to gain an understanding of the strengths and weaknesses of existing processes and systems, such as bottlenecks or discontinuities, as this will be helpful when amending existing processes or designing new ones. This should also reduce the possibility that past inefficient practices will be perpetuated. The views and experience of those currently responsible for existing processes – the process owners – have a crucial role to play in this analysis. At the same time, you need to employ creative thinking to achieve breakthrough and incremental innovation and improvements.

The resulting process maps should identify what amendments or new systems are needed to support change, as well as the skills, competences and knowledge required by those carrying out the processes.

3 Redesign processes

If undertaking a major BPR project, use organisational statements of vision, mission and strategy as a guiding framework; start with the needs of the customer and redesign the processes from the outside in. A range of techniques, including lean management tools, value analysis, Six Sigma and theory of constraints, may be used to facilitate this, reducing inefficiency and waste and creating or increasing added value for stakeholders.

The following guidelines should be applied to the redesign process:

- identify the business processes required to produce particular business outcomes and show clearly how processes interrelate

- identify all the inputs required for each process – raw materials, staff, skills and competences, IT support, equipment

- set out the infrastructure required to support the proposed changes by describing management strategy, measurement systems and reward programmes, as well as the values and belief systems that need to be adopted by all

- improve customer service through genuine empowerment, trust and delegation of responsibility, allowing partnerships to develop with customers and suppliers

- ensure that processes transcend, and are not hindered by, departmental boundaries

- involve all staff, especially those who carry out the processes
- involve external partners, such as suppliers, if their operations are affected
- specify schedules, budgets, completion criteria and economic justifications
- establish new control systems
- build in contingencies for delays or unforeseen problems
- allow for changes in physical location or layout, work flows and organisation structures, plant and IT systems, testing and pilot projects, and redefining roles and responsibilities that will result from the process.

4 IT support systems

IT systems have the potential to simplify project implementation, give greater flexibility and reduce costs. Enterprise resource planning (ERP) systems can help larger organisations to be responsive and proactive in relation to changes in the business environment. However, research indicates that one of the prime causes of the failure of IT systems to deliver the anticipated results is ignoring the human element. In the same way that processes should be built around the customer, IT systems should be built around the end users – that is, the internal customers. The following issues should be considered when introducing new IT systems:

- Systems should be designed to support all business processes, which should not have to be shoehorned into ill-fitting systems.

- Procedures should be easy for end users to understand and put into practice – hence the need to involve employees at the earliest stages of the design process. Thought should be given to the skills, competences and training needed to operate new systems.

- IT should help to facilitate the achievement of individual, departmental and corporate goals.

- The system may need to be tested in parallel with the existing one, possibly over a period of several months. This will put additional pressure on the whole organisation.

5 Establish performance indicators

Improvements in performance can be identified only if you know where you are starting from and what you are aiming to achieve.

Select a balanced mix of traditional hard financial and non-financial measures and softer measures. These may cover such matters as the number of new customers gained or lost, repeat orders, numbers of complaints, attitudes to customers, levels of staff morale, job satisfaction, new skills learned, and so on. Make sure that the three dimensions of process efficiency, product quality and product development times are carefully measured. Reward systems may also need to be realigned to corporate objectives.

6 Plan the implementation

The scale of the implementation plan will again depend on the size and scope of the BPR initiative. For large projects you will need to appoint a project co-ordinator or team, for example.

The following elements should be considered, particularly when undertaking major projects:

- whether implementation will be carried out in one major effort or in two or more phases
- start and finish dates – if possible, try to conduct projects, especially larger ones, during slack periods
- which existing and new processes and systems will be run in parallel before old ones are dropped and when this will happen
- day-by-day schedules for key staff and outline plans for others
- briefing and training for key staff where appropriate
- briefings for external partners, such as suppliers, as to how, and from when, the changes will affect their operations
- notification of customers and other business partners as to how

they will be affected – you may wish to provide details on your website with contact names and details as appropriate

- sufficient time for testing, settling in, tweaking, troubleshooting and general hand-holding – this is likely to be a particularly stressful time for those at the sharp edge

- provision of regular progress reports.

7 Review and maintenance

Remember that process redesign is a continuous process. The performance indicators that have been set should provide a comprehensive overview of how well the changes are working and may identify areas or activities for further development, particularly where strategic objectives are not being met. Allocate adequate resources for continuing maintenance and improvements.

8 The human element

In some case, changes planned as a result of major BPR initiatives may lead to redundancies. Keeping staff informed at all stages reduces the risk of general uncertainty, rumours and fears of further job losses, with the inevitable long-term negative effects on morale and openness to change. Clear policies should be in place both for those being made redundant (if any) and for survivors. Issues to consider include:

- The fair and equitable selection of those who may be made redundant and associated support programmes, including redeployment within or outside the company, counselling, job hunting and redundancy packages.

- The need to demonstrate strong commitment to survivors by rebuilding their confidence, morale, commitment and loyalty through retraining programmes covering the new shape of the organisation, new processes and IT procedures, and new performance and pay systems. Outline what further training and development, counselling and other forms of support are available. Reassure staff regularly.

As a manager you should avoid:

- going for BPR simply because everyone else is doing it
- confusing BPR with downsizing
- assuming you are on the right BPR track merely by introducing the latest IT
- focusing on individual tasks at the expense of the overall process
- embarking on change projects without resources and support to complete – and maintain – them
- introducing BPR only for major business processes.

A programme for benchmarking

Benchmarking is a structured process. It consists of identifying, understanding and adapting the outstanding practices of industry leaders to help an organisation improve its performance and achieve and sustain competitive advantage.

Benchmarking is a powerful tool for organisations seeking continuous improvement. It forms an important part of many change programmes, including total quality management and business process re-engineering. It is a challenging technique that requires careful management and a high level of commitment. When used effectively, it can provide organisations with a continuous competitive advantage, aid the setting or extension of performance goals, focus on and accelerate change, and motivate staff by showing what is possible.

Benchmarking has faced criticism in recent years, however. As with many quality management techniques, there has been a tendency for it to be implemented in an overly formal and mechanistic way that fails to take account of the need for flexibility or give adequate consideration to the human element. Other issues include the amount of time and effort involved (particularly for small organisations), risks around giving away sensitive data, the misuse of statistics and the difficulty of implementing the best practice of others. To avoid these pitfalls, it is important to pay attention to how you are conducting your benchmarking. The tips in the action points below will give you some ideas on how to minimise these problems. However, you also need to consider how to adapt the advice given in the checklist to the specific situation in your organisation.

Another major problem highlighted by critics is that benchmarking discourages innovation because it focuses on encouraging people to achieve the current best practice, rather than promoting a more inventive and original approach to improvement. To counter this, consider using additional quality management techniques such as lean practices to gain fresh ideas.

Various types of benchmarking exist, including:

- internal benchmarking – the measurement and comparison of practices with similar practices in other parts of the organisation
- industry or competitive benchmarking – industry-specific comparisons made either between direct competitors or with target companies making dissimilar products in the same industry
- functional or non-competitive benchmarking – the direct comparison of a function in two or more organisations, which may or may not be in the same industry
- generic or best-practice/world-class benchmarking – benchmarking of the best practice of recognised world-class organisations.

Most organisations use one or a mixture of these approaches. This checklist is intended for managers new to benchmarking or for those wishing to review their current benchmarking practice.

Action checklist

1 Plan your study

Identify the principal business processes within the organisation and the critical success factors needed to achieve the business mission. By mapping these two dimensions in a matrix, weighting the factors that make the biggest impact, you should be able to assess the potential gains to be made from consolidating processes. This will help you decide which areas to benchmark. Focus on those activities that are of real importance to your organisation. Avoid choosing activities that are relatively insignificant and have little impact on business performance, or those that are easy to measure.

Select a small number of related processes to benchmark. Do not be too ambitious at this stage, particularly if this is the first benchmarking project your organisation has undertaken. When selecting processes to benchmark remember the critical success factors: benchmarking activities require the support of senior managers; they should be linked to organisational strategy; and they should be based upon a sound understanding of organisational processes.

Consider the legal and ethical aspects of competitive benchmarking. Confidentiality and data security are important issues for benchmarking partners and groups. This is likely to be one of the senior management team's main concerns, so allay fears beforehand by setting out what information you will share and how you will protect yourself commercially in the process.

2 Identify personnel

Select a benchmarking team and a team leader. Most benchmarking is done by teams to take advantage of the range of skills and knowledge that they can offer. Use an in-place work group, a cross-functional team or a functional team (six members is an average team size). It is helpful to have someone on the team with some experience and/or knowledge of benchmarking.

Although much of the work will be carried out by the benchmarking team, it is advantageous to encourage the participation of all staff, as benchmarking may identify gaps in performance that in turn require radical change anywhere within the organisation. The involvement of process owners from the outset ensures that they are able to play a role in the evaluation process and can become the champions of change. They are also usually the people who know most about the process and its operation in the first place.

It is essential to get the commitment of senior managers at an early stage, as without this it will be difficult to act on the findings of the benchmarking programme and implement any changes that are identified as desirable. If possible, arrange for people with budgetary responsibilities to sponsor the study upfront.

3 Examine the process to be benchmarked

Document the process to be benchmarked to gain an understanding of the activities involved. You need to be clear about what is involved in the process before you attempt to start the benchmarking exercise. Simple flow charts will help you define the inputs and outputs of the process. It is possible that a number of elements could be measured, so take care to determine those that are true indicators of performance. After examining the process, you may have some initial thoughts of your own about how it could be improved; it is up to you whether you make these improvements before benchmarking, or put the process forward for benchmarking as it is already.

4 Data collection

To make a comparison between organisations or parts of an organisation requires data. This may be in the form of statistics, ratios or detailed case studies and descriptions. As the key to the success of the benchmarking project, the data collection process should be carefully planned. Be clear about what you want to measure and define your measurements clearly so that comparison is possible. Only collect the data required for decision-making. Collecting too much data can be as bad as collecting too little.

5 Identify benchmarking partners

Consider internal sources (different departments, divisions or companies within the organisation) and external partners (competitors, similar industries or best-practice/world-class performers). Sources that can help in identifying partners include trade and industry journals, market research reports, government studies, databases, other internet resources, suppliers, customers and corporate networks. Consider contacting a benchmarking clearing house or a joint interest group if these are available in your industry and geographical area.

Solicit the participation of partners. Organisations are often willing to become involved if they can see that they will also benefit from benchmarking, which should be a two-way process. If necessary, appeal to their ego to get them to agree to take part; they have been chosen, after all, because they are an example of excellence. If the form of benchmarking you are undertaking involves several companies, it can be a good opportunity for those companies to form links with one another. You must be willing to share data and findings as well as respecting confidentiality, if requested.

When selecting external partners, take care to choose suitable organisations to compare yourself with – these may be outside your business sector. For example, you may find that a customer service process can be benchmarked with a totally different type of organisation from your own, as the principles are still the same. If you are benchmarking with a number of organisations, be careful to not pick too many, as the workload may become too much to handle effectively.

6 Plan and implement the comparison exercise

Identify the hard and soft issues that need to be measured. Hard issues include ratios, time and costs. Soft issues might include management style, communications, or customer focus.

Prepare an action plan. Identify who will collect the data, from where and when. The benchmarking team should develop an appropriate survey or interview guide. Questionnaires can be administered online, or completed over the telephone or via site visits. Decide which method is the most appropriate for your requirements.

It is easy to underestimate the time needed to collect the data, so err on the side of caution when arranging fact-finding interviews.

7 Collate the data from your organisation and its benchmarking partners

Draw up a matrix of performance indicators from your benchmarking partners (the use of spreadsheets and databases can help in the analysis).

Compare your current performance against the data. Identify where your organisation misses certain targets, fails to match the standards of others, or generally shows room for improvement. The benchmarking team should try to identify the causes of these failures and, with relevant additional staff, make plans to remedy them. It is useful to research case studies of best practice, as they can be used to help you communicate the objectives of change and the benefits that could be achieved.

Involve process owners in setting goals to close, meet and exceed the gaps in performance. The benchmarking team should develop detailed action plans to ensure measures of success are included.

8 Report the findings

When business benefits that could be achieved through change have been identified, communicate the benchmarking findings. You may wish to make a presentation and/or distribute a paper on the exercise to your senior management team. Any information you give them should be concise and clear and should demonstrate how the recommendations will lead to higher performance, better processes and increased competitive advantage.

Consider also how you will communicate the findings to staff. It is probably best to present the information to people in person to make sure they understand it and have an opportunity to ask questions. You could give a dedicated presentation, or you could talk about the benchmarking exercise as part of a regular meeting such as a team meeting or an all-staff briefing. Again, emphasise the positive in a clear fashion and talk about how the changes recommended will help staff in their day-to-day jobs. Demonstrating the benefits will help to gain support for any changes that are needed.

9 Plan improvements and put them into action

Providing that a clear business case can be made, implement the planned improvements, making use of process champions throughout the organisation as catalysts for change. It is at this stage that resources will need to be committed, so this is the point at which you should draw on the senior management support you gained for the project earlier in the process. Improvements should be linked to both organisational strategy and smaller objectives so that they can be achieved by individuals and groups within the organisation. The aim should be to embed the changes so that they are sustained over time rather than enforced as a quick fix. At this stage, you may find it useful to read up on approaches to change management.

10 Monitor and review

Monitor whether the study met its objectives; the impact of the improvements on the organisation; the evidence of a change in the process; the value of the changes to the organisation; and the level of willingness or resistance to change. This will enable you to evaluate the success of the project and decide whether further change is required.

You will now be in a position to select the next process or processes to benchmark. Maintaining momentum is one of the most challenging aspects of benchmarking.

As a manager you should avoid:

- being too ambitious at the start
- being too formal and inflexible in applying benchmarking
- underestimating the need for willingness to change and openness to new ideas

- seeing benchmarking as a tool for providing short-term gains
- dismissing potential benchmarking partners too quickly due to a perceived lack of similarity
- forgetting that benchmarking can fail for a number of reasons, including a lack of commitment, focus or resources.

Genichi Taguchi
Quality engineering

Introduction

Genichi Taguchi (1924–2012) was made an honorary member of the American Society for Quality (ASQ) in May 1998, one of the many awards and commendations bestowed on him. In support of his nomination it was said that his leadership in the quality control field was unsurpassed, and his influence would be felt for a long time in engineering, quality fields and industry sectors throughout the world.

Taguchi is famous for his pioneering methods of modern quality control and low-cost quality engineering. He was the founder of the methodology that has come to be known as the Taguchi method, which seeks to improve product quality at the design stage by integrating quality control into product design through experiment and statistical analysis. His methods have been said to fundamentally change the philosophy and practice of quality control.

Life and career

Born in Japan in 1924, Taguchi initially studied textile engineering until the Second World War, when he joined the Navigation Institute of the Japanese Navy. In 1948 he worked at the Ministry of Public Health and Welfare and the Institute of Statistical Mathematics of the Ministry of Education, where he met Matosaburo Masuyame, a renowned statistician, who nurtured and honed Taguchi's statistical skills. While there he also gained recognition for his contributions to industrial experiments dealing with the production of penicillin.

In 1950, Taguchi joined the Electrical Communication Laboratory (ECL) of Nippon Telephone and Telegraph Company, gaining six years' experience in experimentation and data analysis while developing telephone switching systems. The commercial benefits resulting from his ECL work helped Taguchi win the Deming Prize in 1960 for his contribution to the field of quality engineering. He went on to win this award, one of Japan's most prestigious, three more times.

Taguchi was awarded his doctorate by Kyushu University in 1962, after working with industrial statisticians (and beginning his work on the signal-to-noise ratio) at Bell Laboratories in the US. He continued working for ECL in a consulting role and became part of the associate research staff of the Japanese Standards Association, where he founded the Quality Research Group. In 1964, he took up a professorship at Aoyama Gakuin University in Japan, where he spent the next 17 years developing his methods. Attending some of Taguchi's lectures were the founder of Sony and personnel from a struggling car manufacturer named Toyota.

Throughout this time, Taguchi's methods were largely unheard of outside Japan. He developed his concept of the quality loss function in the early 1970s, but it was during the 1980s that Taguchi methods became established, when he revisited AT&T Bell Laboratories in the US, as director of the Japanese Academy of Quality.

After that, interest from companies such as Xerox, Ford and ITT in his methodology increased. In 1982, Taguchi was involved in seminars for Ford executives, and the next year he became executive director of the Ford Supplier Institute (later known as the American Supplier Institute). He was further honoured in 1986, receiving the Indigo Ribbon from the emperor of Japan for his contribution to Japanese economics and industry (in 1990 he received the Blue Ribbon). He was also awarded the

International Technology Institute's Willard F. Rockwell Medal for combining engineering and statistical methods to achieve rapid improvements in cost and quality by optimising product design and manufacturing processes. Throughout much of this time, Taguchi was operating as a full-time consultant to various major companies in the US, Japan, China and India.

Apart from occasional work with, for example, Lucas Industries, Taguchi's ideas became known in Europe only from 1986, when the Institute of Statisticians organised a conference in London. The UK Taguchi Club (later the Quality Methods Association) was formed the following year. Since then, Taguchi methods have been widely used in the West in a diverse range of industries, although particularly in the car industry. Taguchi died in June 2012

Taguchi methods

Taguchi developed methods for both online (process) and offline (design) quality control. This formed the basis of his approach to total quality control and assurance within a product's development life cycle. His approach emphasised improving the quality of product and process before manufacture (that is, at the design stage), rather than achieving quality through inspection (the more traditional approach).

Quality loss function

Taguchi's approach differed from that of the traditional one of manufacturing a product within a specification based on tolerances equally spaced around a target value. He developed a concept of quality loss occurring as soon as there is a deviation from the target value, and worked in terms of quality loss rather than just quality. He defined quality loss as 'the loss imparted to society from the time the product is shipped', and this related the loss to society as a whole. Thus it included company costs, such as reworking, scrapping and maintenance, and any loss to the customer through poor product performance and lowered reliability.

A loss function curve can be calibrated by using information from the customer. A target value is identified as being the best possible value of a quality characteristic. Taguchi associates a simple, quadratic loss function with deviations from the target. Thus:

- the smaller the performance variation, the better the quality of the product
- the larger the deviation from the target value, the larger the loss to society.

A loss will occur even when the product is within the specification allowed, though it is minimal when the product is on target.

After the design engineer has determined the costs of parts being manufactured out of specification, this information can be used to justify expenditure on quality improvement, enabling decisions to be made on firm cost and quality grounds. Thus the quality gain from changing a design might sometimes be estimated as not worthwhile, though ensuring that a product is produced at a quality level acceptable to the customer remains an important consideration.

Signal-to-noise ratio

One of Taguchi's most innovative ideas was a quality measure called the signal-to-noise ratio, which was used by communications engineers to find the strength of an electrical signal. Taguchi applied this measure to everyday products, and used it as a measure to choose control levels that could best cope with changes in operating and environmental conditions, or noise.

Robust quality of design

On the basis of the signal-to-noise measure Taguchi was able to develop the concept of robustness, which enables a product to be designed to be less affected by noise. Given normal variations in process operations, the product in question would be less likely to fail acceptable quality criteria.

Product design improvement

During the product design and production engineering phases, Taguchi set out three steps that must be followed.

- **System design.** This may involve the development of a prototype design and will determine the materials, parts and assembly system to be used. The manufacturing process also has to be considered.

- **Parameter design.** This aimed to find the most cost-effective way of controlling noise. Taguchi's process and design improvements are gained by identifying easily controllable factors and settings that minimise performance variation. Controllable factors are design factors that a designer can set or easily adjust. The specified value becomes the signal. Uncontrollable factors are noise, or external variations, and a higher signal-to-noise ratio means better quality. Taguchi found that if controllable factors were set at optimal levels, the product would be robust in facing external changes. This was achieved through parameter design applied at the design (offline) stage to reduce or remove the effect of noise factors, and design in robustness. Experiments were designed using orthogonal arrays, which (rather simply described) were a series of rows and columns allowing the effects of different factors to be extracted and separated out. Taguchi was not the inventor of the orthogonal array, but this type of experimentation moved away from the traditional approach of testing one factor at a time and, instead, tested many factors at the same time. His new approach dramatically reduced the number of experiments and prototypes required, and consequently costs were much lower. He developed various experimental designs that allowed the variability of the noise factors on each controllable factor setting to be simulated. The settings that minimised variability could then be determined.

- **Tolerance design.** If parameter design failed, Taguchi suggested using tolerance design to identify the most crucial noise factors. Tolerances could be reassigned so that the overall variability was reduced to acceptable levels.

Invest last not first

Taguchi placed much emphasis on initially optimising the product and process to engineer product quality (parameter design) into the system. Using low-cost materials and components was an important feature of this, and money was spent on higher-cost items only when necessary (tolerance design).

In perspective – from Deming to Taguchi

It was W Edwards Deming who first recognised the importance of moving quality control backwards from inspection to proper process control, notably via statistical process control (SPC). Taguchi moved quality control even further back, to the design stage, thus completing the total quality loop. Taguchi's techniques and statistical experimental designs for offline quality improvement complemented SPC for online quality improvement. Deming's philosophy for management quality improvement encompassed both.

It has been said that Deming's work inspired a revolution in the old management culture while Taguchi inspired evolution. Certainly, Deming provided mainly a theory for management, whereas Taguchi provided important techniques for improving a process at every stage, from design to production, and for keeping the improved processes under control.

Pursuing business excellence

The EFQM (European Foundation for Quality Management) Excellence Model is a non-prescriptive framework based on nine criteria. Five of these are classified as enablers (what an organisation does) and four are classified as results (what it achieves).

In the model, competitive advantage is considered as a natural consequence of an organisation's impact on customers, people and society, and greater business performance can be achieved through the implementation of effective policy and strategy by an organisation's leadership. It provides a framework within which businesses can understand the cause-and-effect relationships between strategies implemented by an organisation and the results it achieves, as Figure 2 shows.

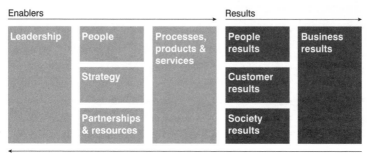

Figure 2: EFQM Model

The updated EFQM Excellence Model was launched in 2012. The framework and nine boxes remain, but one of the boxes has been renamed 'Business results' (formerly 'Key results'). This alteration was made as a consequence of 'key' being interpreted in practice as the most important results. To aid understanding of these criteria, 'business stakeholders' and 'value for money' were also defined to support interpretation across business sectors.

Action checklist

1 Understand the fundamental concepts of excellence

It is important to gain an understanding of the fundamental concepts of excellence and its applicability to the business. The concepts of business excellence are as follows:

- Adding value for customers – organisations that exhibit business excellence focus attention on their customers and seek to understand and develop creative solutions to meet their needs.

- Creating a sustainable future – organisations that show business excellence adopt a holistic approach that includes an understanding of the economic, environmental and social impacts of their operations on their local communities.

- Developing organisational capability – organisations that exhibit business excellence manage change and its consequences effectively.

- Harnessing creativity and innovation – organisations that illustrate business excellence embrace continuous improvement and innovation.

- Leading with vision, inspiration and integrity – organisations that demonstrate business excellence are driven by leaders that envision the future and aspire others to pursue higher purposes.

- Managing with agility – organisations that demonstrate business excellence are flexible and responsive to business opportunities and threats.

- Succeeding through the talent of people – organisations that exhibit business excellence create work environments wherein people are valued and empowered to achieve business and personal objectives.

- Sustaining outstanding results – organisations that demonstrate business excellence consistently achieve results that meet both the short-term and long-term requirements of all stakeholders.

2 Get to know the model

(a) Familiarise yourself with the content and process of the model. Understand how it works and where to start.

The enabler criteria (see Figure 2) deal with the following:

- Leadership: and its required best practice in communication, empowerment, and the way in which change and improvement really work in the organisation.

- People: how the organisation energises the full potential of people to improve their own skills and improve the business.

- Strategy: how organisational values, vision and goals are set.

- Partnerships and resources: how all resources are effectively managed and dealings with partners work to contribute to the achievement of business goals.

- Processes, products and services: how the key processes of supply are turned into products and services that are delivered to the customer.

(b) Consider how best to measure the results criteria that the enablers deliver:

- People results: people's perceptions of the organisation and how their needs and expectations are met.

- Customer results: customers' perceptions of the organisation and how their needs and expectations are met.

- Society results: how the image and position of the organisation are viewed in the community and what the organisation does to try and improve this view.

- Business results: how enablers and results feed into financial results, and how targets are met and reviewed.

  (c) Familiarise yourself with the criterion parts. The nine criteria of points (a) and (b) are further divided into thirty-two criterion parts for purposes of clarifying emphasis and scoring.

  (d) Understand the RADAR (Results, Approaches, Deploy, Assess and Refine) self-assessment framework which requires organisations to:

- determine the Results they wish to achieve
- plan Approaches to achieve these results
- Deploy these approaches systematically
- Assess and Refine the deployed approaches, based on monitoring and analysis of the results achieved.

  This logic should be applied to all the Enablers and Results listed above.

3 Develop commitment throughout the organisation

Get senior management commitment from the start, but make sure that the model becomes a way of working for all employees. Give staff an overview of the model and make clear to them what is involved.

4 Train your employees

You need to have people who understand how the model works, and how to ask the right questions, collect and evaluate the responses, and score them in line with the model. Use external consultants or if necessary train staff in-house.

5 Establish the action teams

You need three preferably separate action teams that are part of the overall project team. They should focus on management overview, data collection and assessment.

6 Decide how you are using the approach

Consider which of the following two options you want to take:

- go for the award – this requires (arguably) an infrastructure that generally only large companies have, although more and more small and medium-sized enterprises are adopting the model

- use the model only as a business improvement tool.

You might find that you do not need to tackle all the criteria, and decide it is best to focus on one particular area. The advantage of using the model in this way is that you can concentrate on areas where organisational efforts will be most rewarded.

7 Decide on the starting point

Some of the enablers may be more contentious or risky than others. Eliciting feedback on managers' effectiveness as leaders or as people managers, for example, may produce some surprises or unpalatable truths. It could be more productive to begin with partnerships and resources, or processes, products and services to get people into the mindset of the model. You might find that by tackling a less contentious issue, the more contentious ones become more approachable.

8 Choose your data-gathering method

Options include:

- surveys requiring yes/no answers
- matrix charts requiring a response on a scale of one to ten
- pro forma charts leading to evidence of achievements and areas to improve.

Make sure you get the questions right. A lot of time can be wasted by asking wrong questions and you may engender resistance.

9 Try some scoring

Advantage may be lost if you do not try to get some hard measures for largely soft issues. Research shows that measurement-conscious companies are stealing a competitive march on those that do not attempt measurement disciplines. Scores may vary wildly from one assessor to another, strengthening the case for training people and persevering with scores over time.

10 Find out where you are

Writing up the summary report (including scores and comments from feedback) will give you a good idea of how much there is to tackle. This provides the basis for generating and prioritising the plan for business improvement. If you decide to go for full implementation, the business improvement plan will be a key component in compiling the report to be submitted for examination by the EFQM.

As a manager you should avoid:

- starting with issues likely to be contentious
- failing to identify the key questions to ask before starting to gather data
- failing to develop measures for 'soft' issues.

Preparing for ISO 9001 registration

ISO 9001 is a quality management standard setting out requirements for managing quality across an organisation. It provides a framework that enables an organisation to develop a quality management system to suit its own situation regardless of the nature of its business. The standard is based on eight management principles: customer focus; leadership; the involvement of people across the organisation; effective business processes; a system approach to management; a commitment to continual improvement; a factual approach to decision-making; and mutually beneficial supplier relationships. It also provides a guide to measuring the effectiveness of the quality management system and making use of those measures to promote continual improvement.

ISO 9001 is, perhaps, the world's most widely used and well-recognised quality management tool, with over one million certificates issued in 184 countries and economies in 2012. First introduced by the International Organization for Standardization (ISO) in 1987 as a successor to BS 5750, the ISO 9000 series of standards is designed to help organisations, both large and small, from all sectors, to ensure efficiency and consistency in their operations.

Based around eight management principles, ISO 9001 provides a model with which organisations can build a quality management system, integrating quality initiatives that might otherwise be approached in isolation from each other. ISO 9001 is a tool for organisational improvement that can be used to enhance and simplify processes by examining what is done and how it is done, and by promoting an increased awareness of customers' needs and expectations. Once organisations have developed quality management systems that meet the criteria for ISO 9001, they can apply for registration through a nationally recognised accreditation body.

The benefits of ISO 9001 accreditation include better quality management, improved operational performance, more efficient processes, productivity improvements, cost savings, a greater ability to meet customer needs and better customer service. Accreditation can also enhance an organisation's reputation by demonstrating adherence to quality standards, and help to maintain or open up business opportunities with partners who require their suppliers to be accredited.

However, ISO 9001, along with many other quality management approaches, has also been criticised for being overly bureaucratic and process-focused rather than outcome-driven. It is also sometimes perceived as more relevant to manufacturing and industry rather than the services sector. Proponents of ISO 9001 would counter these critiques by arguing that the way that ISO 9001 is implemented has a strong bearing upon how successful it is. This checklist discusses what you can do to increase the effectiveness of ISO 9001 in your organisation. ISO 9001 should be the beginning not the end of quality management in your organisation, and you will need to think about what more you can do to improve standards.

A new draft of the ISO 9001 standards has been published, and the final updated version is expected by the end of 2015. This will include a number of changes such as an increased focus on risk, the use of the same high-level structure used by other management system standards, a requirement for senior management to actively align quality policies with business needs, and some changes to terminology. This checklist is intended for managers involved in the implementation of a quality management system within their organisation, based on the ISO 9000 series of standards, and describes the processes involved.

Action checklist

1 Buy and read the standard and relevant guidelines

The ISO 9000 series of standards outlines the requirements for a quality management system, with ISO 9000:2008 giving the full specification. For reference, ISO 9000:2005 defines the terms and vocabulary used, and ISO 9004:2009 outlines how to make the quality management system more efficient and effective.

The standard allows organisations to tailor some of the requirements to suit their circumstances. For example, parts of the product realisation section can be omitted if they are not appropriate to the organisation or the product or service, or are not required by customers. All other sections of the standard are mandatory. Any reason for exclusion must be clearly defined and qualified within the quality manual (see point 10).

2 Gain senior management commitment

The standard places responsibility on senior management to manage the system. They must understand their customers' needs at a strategic level and be able to translate this into policies and objectives to meet them. They must also make sure that there are clear paths of communication throughout the organisation, and that all staff are aware of customers' needs. There is a requirement for senior management to regularly review the effectiveness of the quality management system.

3 Decide how the organisation will be registered and select an assessment body

It is possible for part of an organisation to apply for registration. If there is just a single site, consider whether all departments should be accredited. If it is a multi-site organisation, you can either apply for multi-site accreditation or accredit each site individually.

Consider the cost implications of your decision and be careful to adopt a unified approach across the organisation, working within the guidelines of ISO 9001. It is better for diverse sites to work towards accreditation together, irrespective of the product or service they deliver.

Although registration comes at the end of the process, one of the first tasks will be to select an assessment body. In the UK it is advisable to select a body approved by the United Kingdom Accreditation Service (UKAS). It is also usually best to have the development process and the accreditation assessment carried out by separate bodies, rather than by the same one.

4 Appoint a management representative

The management representative will be a member of the organisation's management team who holds overall day-to-day responsibility for the administration of the quality management system. The appointee must be a member of the organisation's own staff and not an external consultant, and will provide a link with the assessment body both during and between assessment visits. Sustained management commitment and good communication between management and employees are key contributors to the success of ISO 9001, so making a suitable appointment is crucial. The alignment of quality with strategy by senior management is a new requirement under the proposed changes to ISO 9001, indicating the importance of management in the ISO 9001 process.

5 Decide whether outside help is required

Depending on the resources and knowledge available within your organisation, you may wish to employ outside help to assist in the ISO 9001 registration process. Some trade organisations are able to provide assistance, and there are many organisations providing training courses in ISO 9001 and quality management techniques. Employing outside help will add to the cost of registration, but this must be weighed against the benefits and expertise provided.

6 Involve staff

It is crucial to gain the commitment of all staff. Be prepared for resistance to change when first introducing ISO 9001. Some staff may see the standard as overly bureaucratic, as a threat to their working practices, or as something that will draw attention to individuals when mistakes are made. It is important to allay any such fears and to emphasise that the aim is not to single people out for blame, but to improve the quality of products and services through the simplification and rationalisation of processes. Emphasise that every member of staff has an important contribution to make.

It can be helpful to appoint a team with members from different areas of the organisation to assist in shaping the project. Team members will be able to pool their expertise and act as advocates for the project in their own departments.

7 Interpret the requirements

There are eight sections in ISO 9001:2008, each with a number of sub-sections. The first three are for definition only. The remaining five are operational and are as follows:

- Section 4: Quality Management System – this looks at processes and how they interact and specifies the documentation needed to manage the system effectively.

- Section 5: Management Responsibility – how top management will manage the system.

- Section 6: Resource Management – how the organisation's resources are utilised to carry out the processes.

- Section 7: Product Realisation – how input is converted into output.

- Section 8: Measurement, Analysis, Improvement – how an organisation measures the performance of the quality management system and how these measures are used for continual improvement.

You will need to think through how these relate to your organisation.

8 Write a quality policy

A quality policy is the foundation upon which all quality activities are based. It is a mission statement and it must come from senior management. The quality policy should be kept simple, to enable it to be understood by all staff, and should confirm the requirements of the standard and its objectives and goals for quality, including the requirement to meet customer expectations and needs. Under ISO 9001:2008, it is mandatory to have a quality policy.

9 Draw up a project plan

Once the objectives have been established, the next step is to draw up a project plan. This should cover the allocation of responsibilities and resources and set out how you will establish effective processes to meet objectives. Think, too, about any training and development needed to ensure that staff are competent to implement the system. The plan will also enable you to build and chart progress. All those involved should meet and review progress at regular intervals to maintain impetus. Take care to set a realistic timetable.

10 Map processes and document the quality management system

ISO 9001 provides a set of requirements for managing work. Processes across the organisation need to be mapped and documented, typically focusing on areas such as sales, product or service development, purchasing, production and service delivery. This provides a key to understanding the flow of work through the organisation and ultimately will show where improvements can be made. It is important to focus on the interaction of processes across the organisation, as well as the competence of staff carrying them out. One helpful approach is to start with a customer request and map the fulfilment journey and the processes involved.

Processes are often represented graphically using some form of flow chart, clearly showing the relationships and the flow of work. Remember that any process will have three stages: input, operation and output.

ISO 9001 requires the production of a quality manual as well as operational procedures. The quality system may be recorded in any medium you choose, providing there is clear evidence of control to prevent unauthorised changes. Certain operational procedures must be documented and maintained: control of documents; control of records; internal audits; control of non-conforming product or service; corrective action and preventive action. Some of these are discussed in more detail below.

11 Establish performance indicators

A framework must be established to measure the effectiveness of the quality management system. Select realistic and measurable indicators, such as the length of time taken to answer a customer query, output rates and reject quantities. Define how indicators are to be measured and set targets to be achieved. Monitor performance against targets regularly. If these targets are linked with performance management within the organisation, they are more likely to be successful. For example, if quality management targets are discussed at performance appraisals or taken into account in the consideration of promotions, employees will take them more seriously.

12 Use complaints positively

Establish or enhance your existing complaints system by treating each complaint (be it from external or internal sources) as an indicator of a need for improvement. Positive action is required to correct any fault in the short term and eliminate the cause in the longer term. This is known as corrective action. Action taken to prevent a fault from occurring in the first place is called preventive action. It is mandatory that you have a procedure for dealing with corrective and preventive actions under ISO 9001:2008. Whatever happens, make sure that you keep the complainant informed of progress.

13 Review the system

Monitoring, measurement and review are essential, but allow a
reasonable amount of time before conducting a review of the
system and establish an audit programme covering the whole
organisation. Quality audits are an important review tool; they
examine organisational processes and procedures and compare
what is actually being done with the standard that has been set.
Anomalies found in an audit not only point out deviations from
the agreed procedure but may also indicate areas for further
improvements. Examine and act upon any trends in the number
and type of non-conformities.

14 Prepare for assessment

When you are satisfied that the quality management system
has begun to achieve the goals and objectives set in the
quality policy, and when there has been sufficient time to
obtain appropriate documentary records, you can apply for
certification. You may wish to consider pre-assessment; some
assessment bodies offer a pre-assessment visit to enable
potential discrepancies to be addressed. If this is not feasible,
conduct an independent audit of the whole system. It is possible
that a first assessment may highlight a number of discrepancies,
probably of a minor nature, but each one has the potential to
prevent successful registration. Only when you are satisfied that
your quality management system is performing as you and the
standard require should you arrange for an assessment visit.

15 Assessment

This will be comprehensive, and may last for two or three
days, so be prepared to devote time to the assessment team.
Assessments start with an opening meeting where the assessors
explain what they are looking for and the actions they will take if
discrepancies are found.

The main assessment normally consists of two parts: a
documentation audit and an implementation audit. In the first,

the assessors will look at whether the procedures and controls required by the standard have been satisfactorily developed; in the second, they will look for evidence to show that what has been written down is actually being practised and that processes and controls are working effectively. The visit will conclude with a meeting at which the assessors will present their report and identify any changes or corrections that need to be made. Depending on the nature and number of discrepancies found, they may or may not recommend registration. Occasionally the assessors may recommend that serious non-conformities are addressed before registration, in which case a second visit may be required.

16 Maintaining registration

Once you have been awarded ISO 9001 registration, it is important to maintain a constant check on your quality management system through audits and review meetings. An assessor from the chosen accreditation body will undertake an annual surveillance visit, with a recertification audit taking place every third year. Lastly, remember that a quality management system is flexible, not set in stone.

As a manager you should avoid:

- writing all the procedures yourself
- allowing the process to become excessively bureaucratic
- failing to involve customers and suppliers in the process
- being afraid to change anything that is not proving effective.

Joseph M Juran
Quality management

Introduction

Joseph M Juran (1904–2008) was a charismatic figure, acknowledged worldwide for his extensive contribution to quality management. Although Juran is often referred to as one of the leading figures of total quality management, much of his work preceded the total quality concept. He became a legend in his own time, and has been instrumental in shaping many of our current ideas about quality. He is recognised, along with W Edwards Deming, as greatly accelerating the development of the quality movement in Japan. His influence on manufacturing throughout the world has been substantial.

Life and career

Juran was born in a small village in Romania in 1904. He was the third of four children and lived in poverty for much of his childhood. His father left the family in 1909 to find work in the US, and some three years later there was enough money for the rest of the family to join him in Minnesota.

Juran excelled at school and his affinity for mathematics and science meant that he soon advanced the equivalent of three year grades. He enrolled at the University of Minnesota in 1920 and became the first member of his family to enter higher education. By 1924 he had earned a degree in electrical engineering, and in 1936 he got a degree in law at Loyola University. During his career Juran produced many international handbooks, training courses and training books that have all been well received and have collectively been translated into sixteen languages. He was awarded more than forty honorary doctorates, honorary memberships, medals and plaques around the world. For his work on quality in Japan, he was awarded the Second Order of the Sacred Treasure for 'the development of quality control in Japan and the facilitation of US and Japanese friendship'; and in the US he was awarded the National Medal of Technology.

Starting out as a professional engineer in 1924, Juran worked in the inspection department at the famous Hawthorne works of Western Electric, and this first job stimulated his interest in quality. The plant was vast, with some 40,000 workers, 5,000 of whom were involved in inspection. Juran's prodigious memory enabled him to develop an encyclopaedic knowledge of the place. His intellectual and analytical abilities were soon recognised, and he quickly progressed through a series of line-management and staff jobs.

In 1926 a team of statistical quality control pioneers from Bell Laboratories came to the Hawthorne plant to apply some of their methods and techniques. Juran was selected as one of twenty people to participate in the training programme and was later appointed as one of the two engineers in the newly formed inspection statistical department. It was while in this role that he authored his first work, *Statistical Methods Applied to Manufacturing Problems*.

By 1937 Juran was head of industrial engineering at Western Electric's head office in New York. He became the equivalent of an in-house consultant, visiting other companies and discussing ideas about quality and industrial engineering. Indeed, it was on one such visit to General Motors in Detroit that he realised how relevant Pareto's idea about 'the vital few and the trivial many' were to quality management, and he eventually described this idea as the Pareto principle (see below).

In 1941 Juran was seconded as an assistant administrator to the

Lend-Lease Administration in Washington. This assignment was to last for four years, during which he streamlined the shipment process to reduce the number of documents required and significantly cut costs. Today such an approach might be called business process re-engineering – Juran long claimed that there was nothing new about BPR.

Juran left Washington and Western Electric in 1945 with the aim of writing, lecturing and consulting. In 1951 he published his *Quality Control Handbook*, which established his reputation as an authority on quality and increased demand for his lecturing and consulting services. In 1954 he delivered a series of lectures in Japan at the invitation of the Union of Japanese Scientists and Engineers. In Japan, it is widely held that these lectures formed the basis of the country's shift towards an economy based on quality principles. Juran himself played down their significance, saying that Japan would have achieved world-quality leadership 'all the same'. The ideas from these lectures were published in his book *Managerial Breakthrough* in 1964.

He founded the Juran Institute in 1979, with the aim of increasing awareness of his ideas. It was through this institute that the widely acclaimed video series *Juran on Quality Improvement* was produced. Juran also played a part in setting up the Malcolm Baldrige National Quality Award and retired from leading the institute only in 1987. He continued to publish into the 1990s and was working on another textbook before he died in February 2008, at the age of 103.

Key ideas

Pareto principle

In his early days as a young engineer, Juran noted that when a list of defects was arranged in order of frequency, relatively few types of defects accounted for the bulk of those found. As his career in management progressed, he noted the occurrence of this phenomenon in other areas. The idea of 'the vital few and the trivial many' was forming. In the 1930s Juran was introduced to the work of Vilfredo Pareto, an Italian economist, who had produced a mathematical model to explain the unequal distribution of wealth. Pareto had not promoted his model as a universal one and did not talk of an 80:20 split, but in preparing the first edition of the *Quality Control Handbook* Juran needed a form of shorthand to describe his idea. Remembering Pareto's work, he captioned his description as 'Pareto's principle of unequal distribution'. Since then the Pareto principle has become a standard term to describe any situation where a small percentage of factors are responsible for a substantial percentage of effect. Juran later published an explanation of his error in attributing more to Pareto than the latter had originally claimed, at the same time recognising the contribution of another economist, M O Lorenz. Juran was, in reality, the first to identify and popularise the 80:20 rule (as it has colloquially become known) as a universal principle.

Breakthrough

In his classic work, *Managerial Breakthrough*, Juran presents his general theory of quality control. Central to this was the idea of an improvement breakthrough.

Juran defines a breakthrough as 'change, a dynamic, decisive movement to new, higher levels of performance'. This he contrasts with control, which means 'staying on course, adherence to standard, prevention of change'. Not all control is viewed as negative and not all breakthroughs are expected to be for the good. Breakthrough and control are seen as part of a continuing cycle of events. Juran highlighted the importance of managers' understanding of the attitudes, the organisation and the methodology used to achieve breakthrough, and of how they differ from those used to achieve control.

The Juran trilogy and quality planning road map

Juran's message on quality covers a number of different aspects. He focused on the wider issues of planning and organisation, managerial responsibility for quality, and the importance of setting targets for improvement. Intrinsic to these, however, was his belief that quality does not happen by accident and needs to be planned. The process of quality improvement is best summarised in his 'trilogy' concept, based on the three financial management processes of financial planning, financial control and financial improvement. Various interpretations of the trilogy have been published; Table 1 represents one version.

Table 1: The Juran trilogy

Quality planning	Identify who the customers are Determine the needs of those customers Translate those needs into our language Optimise the product features so as to meet our needs and customer needs
Quality control	Develop a process that is able to produce the product Optimise the process
Quality improvement	Prove that the process can produce the product under operating conditions Transfer the process to operations

Juran's road map provides a more detailed approach to the steps within the quality planning element of the trilogy. It is made up of a series of actions with corresponding outputs, and emphasises the need for measurement throughout. In his book, *Juran on Quality by Design*, he describes these activities in the road map: establish quality goals; identify the customer; determine customer needs; develop product features; develop process features; establish process controls; and transfer to operations.

Quality campaigns

Juran was never a fan of quality campaigns based on slogans and praise. He viewed the Western quality crisis of the early 1980s as being a result of too many quality initiatives based on campaigns with too little planning and substance. In his view, planning and action should make up 90% of an initiative, with the remaining 10% being exhortation.

Juran's formula for success is:

- establish specific goals to be reached
- establish plans for reaching those goals
- assign clear responsibility for meeting the goals
- base the rewards on the results achieved.

In perspective

Juran's contribution to the revolution in Japanese quality philosophy helped transform Japan into a market leader. This, together with his influence on Western manufacturing and management in general, made him a guru who was influential for more than half a century.

Juran had a varied career in management. And although his fame centres on his ideas and thinking on quality issues, his influence in the field of management is far wider. He played a number of roles – writer, teacher, trainer and consultant – and contributed a great deal, over many years, to the field of management. Many of the thousands of managers who have learned from him hold him in near-reverence, and management today is infused with his techniques and ideas, even though the name of their creator is not always recognised.

Six Sigma

Six Sigma is an approach to improving efficiency and quality by measuring defects or variations in manufacturing and business processes. It compares the output of a process with customer requirements and uses detailed process analysis and statistical tools to understand the root causes of process variation. In contrast to lean thinking, which focuses on cutting out unnecessary steps in the creation of products or the delivery of services, Six Sigma aims to reduce variations or defects so as to streamline processes and eliminate waste. The use of Six Sigma creates value for the customer through a systematic approach to continuous improvement, process improvement and process redesign.

Six Sigma offers a structured and disciplined method for improving the efficiency of processes in organisations. It is data- and fact-driven, involving the collection and detailed analysis of information to provide quantifiable evidence of improvements. It has a relentless focus on the customer, defining and measuring performance to customer requirements.

The term Six Sigma is a registered trademark of Motorola, a telecommunications company that reintroduced the techniques of statistical process control into total quality management (TQM) and rebranded the system as Six Sigma. Motorola implemented the technique successfully in the 1980s. Six Sigma is based on the statistical tools and techniques of quality management developed by Joseph Juran.

Some organisations have used Six Sigma to make sustainable improvements in efficiency and productivity, and it has also been found to be useful in managing innovation, as well as motivating employees, increasing customer satisfaction, and achieving significant bottom-line results. However, Six Sigma has not always been successful in practice and has its critics. Some see it as overly rigorous, time-consuming and mechanistic in its approach to change and improvement, neglecting or ignoring softer political and behavioural issues. Others suggest that its emphasis on reducing process variations hinders innovation, focuses too much on easy gains and has little long-term success. The high cost of the training, qualifications and accreditation offered by commercial providers has also been criticised. Lastly, some find the use of statistical techniques and Japanese terminology intimidating and off-putting.

Interpretations of Six Sigma vary. Some organisations use the term as a label for their company-wide approach to quality, and others use it purely as a measurement and improvement device. There are also numerous versions of Six Sigma and Design for Six Sigma (DFSS). DFSS is used on new processes but is not universally recognised and does not have a methodology; it is also defined differently by different organisations. The DMAIC (design, measure, analyse, improve, control – see point 4 below) methodology is the most universally recognised approach to Six Sigma, and it is used on existing processes within an organisation.

Six Sigma tools and techniques are often used within a broader, overarching organisational framework. Although the two approaches to improving efficiency are very different, Six Sigma is increasingly used in conjunction with the principles of lean thinking. Some organisations have attempted to address the limitations of Six Sigma by combining it with organisation development methods or a strengths-based approach, which focuses on how to build on what is working well and how to learn from cases of positive deviance from existing processes.

Action checklist

1 Gain an understanding of Six Sigma concepts and principles

Before an organisation can contemplate introducing Six Sigma, its managers need to understand exactly what it is. As with any quality initiative, it is crucial to secure the understanding and commitment of senior management before proceeding. Advice from consultants on the use of short training sessions is usually necessary.

Sigma is a Greek letter used in mathematics to denote standard deviation, or the extent to which a process varies from the mean. As the level of sigma rises, the level of variation decreases. The term Six Sigma refers to 3.4 defects per million opportunities. In fact, 3.4 defects/million occurs at 4.5 sigma, i.e. +/– 4.5 standard deviations from the norm. Motorola justifies this 1.5 shift by referring to the occurrence of process drift over a long period.

Six Sigma techniques hinge on a continuous reduction of process variation. This is achieved by first defining and measuring variation in each process, and then discovering its root causes. This enables the development of operational means to control and reduce the level of variation. Four or five Six Sigma tools are typically used, namely, failure mode and criticality analysis (FMCA), cost of poor quality, the five Whys, root cause analysis and variance analysis.

Six Sigma involves not only reducing existing variation, but also avoiding any future variations that might develop. With this in mind, designers need to design for producibility, making all new processes and products as little subject to variance as possible. This can be achieved by such methods as 'poka-yoke' or mistake-proofing, which aim to design processes with minimal opportunities for error and halt processes operating under conditions that will lead to defects. In addition, any potential problems for the organisation should be assessed and guarded against. Techniques such as total preventive maintenance and risk assessments are used for this.

Six Sigma is best used to measure variation in repeatable environments, whether in a manufacturing or a service context. A service environment, for example, where there are many transactions, would be suitable for Six Sigma.

2 Select and train key personnel

Project teams need to be formed with the brief of implementing Six Sigma in different areas and empowered to deliver tangible business results for the whole organisation. Key team members will need to be trained in leadership skills. Training in Six Sigma techniques is almost always carried out by external training providers. It traditionally involves three stages:

- **Green Belt.** Participants earn the status of Green Belt by completing a short course that introduces the Six Sigma methodology.

- **Black Belt.** Some Green Belts, usually of managerial status, proceed to complete a project exercise using the knowledge they have gained. Black Belts will hold responsibility for leading and developing the teams, advising management and teaching Six Sigma techniques to team members.

- **Master Black Belt.** A select few will need further training that will make them the organisation's Six Sigma experts, leading the whole initiative, integrating it into the organisation's strategic plans and teaching the techniques to others.

Different terminology can be used for these levels of training, and it is important to use names that resonate in your particular organisation. Certification is usually given for each level of training, but this is not yet supported by an international standard.

3 Identify appropriate Six Sigma projects

Opportunities for improvement may be identified by assessing organisational performance measurements and scorecards and through workshops or brainstorming sessions. Once a list of ideas has been generated it is important to evaluate them, as not all will be suitable for Six Sigma projects. Criteria to consider include scope, business criticality, anticipated benefits and complexity. Taking into account the resources available, assess the feasibility of individual projects and prioritise those that appear to have the highest impact on customer value, or, initially at least, those in areas where improvements can be made relatively quickly, in order to showcase success. Several projects may be carried out each year.

4 Bring the Six Sigma teams into action

Assign projects to teams with an appropriate level of training and experience. Each team will apply statistical techniques to their project following an agreed framework.

The DMAIC (define, measure, analyse, improve, control) process improvement methodology is used here. The five stages are as follows:

- **Define.** The team focuses on defining the project goals and identifying processes that customers perceive as value-creating. They then need to work out what a perfect process would be. For example, a delivery company might aim to deliver all parcels by noon on the day after dispatch.

- **Measure.** The next step is to measure how the process is performing in reality. The common measurement used is defects per unit, which can be applied to virtually any process in any area of the company. For example, a unit might be a line of computer code, a sales invoice, a piece of raw material, a finished product, a delivery, or a record in a database. In the above example, a unit is a parcel delivered on schedule, and a defect occurs when the parcel fails to be delivered on time.

- **Analyse.** Develop a causal hypothesis and identify the vital few root causes, then move on to validate the hypothesis.

- **Improve.** Develop ideas to remove the root causes and test solutions, finding better ways to do things. Implement these using project management techniques. If, for example, the parcel was not delivered on time because of traffic congestion, one way of avoiding this kind of failure might be to investigate alternative routes around the city.

● **Control.** Establish standard measures to maintain performance.

Additional tools and techniques are used in each of the DMAIC stages. These may include process mapping, data collection forms, control charts, flow diagrams, Pareto charts, the balanced scorecard, voice of the customer, failure modes and effects analysis (FMEA), process variance analysis and creative thinking.

5 Integrate Six Sigma into organisational infrastructure

If Six Sigma is to become a company-wide initiative, it needs to be integrated with existing company structures and practices. Consider introducing links to pay and rewards, departmental budgets, job descriptions and documentation such as ISO 9001. Modify policies and procedures to reflect the improvements made.

At this stage you may wish to consider incorporating the guiding principles of lean management, such as:

● value – as defined from the viewpoint of the customer

● the elimination of waste – redundancy in processes and materials

● continuous improvement – by learning from experience and feedback

● holistic optimisation – improvements at the big-picture level

● build for quality – building in a focus on quality first as part of the process.

6 Monitor and evaluate success

Make sure that projects are monitored, and that successes are publicised and failures investigated. Ascertain not only what cost savings and returns have been achieved, but also whether employee job satisfaction and customer satisfaction have improved.

Remember that customer demands, marketplaces and business environments are dynamic and changing. Periodically reassess processes that have already been analysed to see whether changes are needed because of changed circumstances.

As a manager you should avoid:

- focusing only on the short term – a longer-term focus on customers will be more successful

- allowing yourself to be daunted by the inclusion of statistical techniques – training will be provided and software can perform the calculations

- restricting access to performance data to managerial levels – it will need to be freely available to everyone

- forgetting to teach the soft skills required for handling meetings, teamworking and facilitation – these are needed to ensure that statistical analysis is carried out efficiently

- dismissing Six Sigma as unsuitable for smaller companies – it may cost proportionately more to get started in small companies, but it can still lead to long-term improvements.

Lean transformation

The term lean production was coined by John Krafcik, a researcher at the International Motor Vehicle Programme (IMVP) at the Massachusetts Institute of Technology (MIT). Lean is a management philosophy that focuses organisational effort on understanding and improving customer value with fewer resources through the elimination of waste.

In their book *The Machine that Changed the World* (1991), James Womack and Daniel Jones identified five principles of lean:

- Specify what creates value from the customer's perspective.
- Identify all steps across the whole value stream.
- Make those actions that create value flow.
- Make just in time only what is ordered by the customer.
- Strive for perfection by continually removing successive layers of waste.

Lean is about less waste, shorter cycle times and reduced bureaucracy, higher levels of employee knowledge and engagement, improved organisational agility and higher productivity.

The concept of lean production became popular in the 1990s following the publication of Womack and Jones's book, although its roots go back to developments in Japanese industry in the 1950s and 1960s. Womack and Jones highlighted the significant performance gap between Western and Japanese manufacturers in the automobile sector and explored the techniques used by successful companies such as the Toyota Motor Corporation in Japan. Toyota developed a complete lean production system called the Toyota Production System, which has become known as The Toyota Way. Since the 1990s lean production, or lean enterprise, or just lean, as it is more commonly known today, has emerged as an improvement philosophy that has relevance for all sectors.

Lean is essentially a management philosophy concerned with relentless, sustained improvement (*kaizen*) and the removal of waste (*muda*). Any expenditure of resource – materials, people, or time – that does not add value to the customer is considered to be waste and should be removed. Value must be viewed from the customer's perspective and can be deemed to be any action or process for which customers would be willing to pay. Lean organisations understand customer value and focus attention on continuous improvement.

Research by the Lean Enterprise Research Centre suggests that for most manufacturing production operations, typically only 5% of activities actually add value, 35% are necessary non-value-adding activities and 60% add no value at all. Eliminating non-value-adding activities (or waste) is thus the greatest potential source of improvement in customer service and corporate performance.

Originally emerging as an approach to improving the efficiency of manufacturing operations, lean principles can be, and are, applied to organisations in any sector. There are numerous examples of how lean principles have been applied in service industries including healthcare, call centres, financial services and retail. Lean principles can be used in the service sector with little adaptation of the techniques originally developed for the manufacturing environment. Lean principles can also be applied in a variety of contexts, from small projects and initiatives through to organisation-wide programmes of change.

This checklist covers the management activities that need to be considered when implementing a lean transformation within an organisation. It introduces a range of lean management principles and techniques, but managers are encouraged to undertake wider reading and training to gain a fuller understanding. This checklist focuses on organisation-wide implementation, but many of the issues raised also need to be addressed in smaller lean initiatives.

Action checklist

1 Gain an understanding of the concept of lean

Lean is a concept that means different things to different groups of people. For managers it is often one of those areas where a little knowledge is a dangerous asset. Researching and reading around the concept of lean will help you develop your understanding of its depth and scope and think about an appropriate application for your organisation. Consider the wider resources available to you. Talk to colleagues in your networks and seek out case-study organisations so that you can learn from their experience. From your research you should gain an understanding of the principles of lean as defined above and form a view as to what they might mean for your organisation.

2 Recognise that lean applies across the enterprise

Because of its origins, lean has often been seen as an approach that can only be applied to manufacturing activities and cannot be relevant in other sectors. There are now many detailed examples of the successful application of lean in service-based organisations, demonstrating that this is no longer a valid stance. The implementation of lean covers all areas of an organisation, including all internal functions.

Lean should not be approached as an activity that relates to just one or two sections of an organisation. Any activity has the potential to be inefficient or wasteful of resources. The aim should be for all activities within the organisation to create value, not just those at the forefront of customer service.

Lean practices improve overall business performance by:

- reducing the time spent in performing business activities
- reducing the total cost of doing business by eliminating wasted time and effort
- increasing customer satisfaction through the improved quality and timeliness of deliverables
- improving employee morale and increasing enthusiasm by engaging staff in the development and implementation of improvements.

3 Be aware that lean transformation must start with the senior team

An organisation-wide lean transformation programme is a strategic initiative that should be pursued because it makes good business and financial sense for the organisation. It is, however, as much about transforming people and culture as about streamlining processes. The transformation should be led from the top. As is the case with many change projects, lean transformation may face resistance from people across the organisation. Strong leadership is required to drive the initiative forward and to keep people focused on the main objectives. Hence senior manager commitment across the organisation is critical to success.

4 Provide a compelling case for the initiative

Lean is a strategic initiative, and to be successful you will need a strategic statement that outlines your vision and the goals you are setting. This needs to be brief and engaging for employees, as lean involves encouraging everyone to rethink the way they work. Your objective is to remove all waste from your value-adding activities and your strategy needs to outline the defining parameters to achieve this. Aim high and seek to establish best-in-class targets. Establishing incremental targets will lead people to think that only minor adjustments are needed. Big goals require more radical thinking and are more engaging and rewarding for teams when achieved.

5 Recognise that lean must be embedded in the culture of your organisation

It is crucial to understand the existing culture of an organisation before introducing any programme of change. Leaders and managers will be better placed to implement strategy and achieve their goals if they are aware of the culture of their organisation and the way in which it needs to change. Strategies that are inconsistent with organisational culture are more likely to fail, and those that are in line with it are more likely to succeed. Likewise, an understanding of organisational culture is essential for the effective leadership of lean transformations.

Recognise that understanding and applying the tools and techniques of lean is only a small part of the equation. The human element plays a substantial role in any lean initiative. Lean is not just about applying a number of new techniques; it is just as much about focusing on the way teams go about their work, how they approach their activities, become critical and analytical, continuously seek improvements and learn and develop in their roles.

The transition to a true lean culture should not be seen as a short-term fix. For many people and in many organisations, lean is a new way of thinking which can take years to embed into the culture. Look for short-term gains and successes, but remain committed to the long term and be prepared to invest the necessary time and resources to ensure your culture evolves in the right way.

A lean culture is one where:

- the customer is the focus of all activity
- the search for continuous improvement is strong
- a clear customer-focused vision is identified by senior managers
- clear expectations and standards are set so that everyone understands their role.

The Toyota Production System (TPS) developed by the Toyota

Motor Corporation is a good example of how the removal of all forms of waste can be embedded into the culture of the organisation. The TPS lies in at the heart of the organisation and is described by Toyota as 'a production system which is steeped in the philosophy of the complete elimination of all waste imbuing all aspects of production in pursuit of the most efficient methods'. The values, principles and manufacturing ideals known as The Toyota Way are passed on from generation to generation in the company. The Toyota Way, in turn, is driven by *kaizen* and the principles of valuing and developing people. As a precursor to lean, its success lies in the fact that the philosophy has become deeply embedded in the culture of the organisation.

6 Engage your teams

As with any change initiative, getting employee buy-in to the project will be critical to success. People put up barriers to change when there is uncertainty, a lack of understanding of the need for change, or poor communication. Many staff will have experienced numerous change initiatives that have had varying degrees of success.

People are usually more receptive to change and will engage with lean if they:

- understand the failings of the current approach
- recognise that the current situation is unsustainable
- believe that now is the time to change
- are clear about what the change will involve
- are confident in their ability to implement the changes
- believe that everyone is working to deliver success.

Good communications are essential to the success of lean projects, so include representatives from all functions and levels of the organisation in the planning process. Lean is about cultural change and employee participation, and ownership is an essential part of accepting the change process. Arrange meetings, briefing sessions and newsletters to promote the objectives of lean.

7 Identify lean champions

Having gained the commitment of senior management, you must plan how to roll out lean to different parts of the organisation. You should begin with people, and lean champions can make a significant contribution to success. A lean champion is someone who can drive lean transformation forward at a strategic, departmental or team level. Most often they are people who understand the business processes in their area of responsibility, have a clear awareness of the total operations of the business and are committed to continuous improvement.

Lean champions must be able to:

- gain the respect of the rest of their team
- understand the lean techniques that the organisation is adopting
- lead, facilitate and manage lean projects
- train and coach the team in the use of lean tools
- produce documents such as process maps and progress reports
- demonstrate enthusiasm and keep the momentum going.

Lean champions can exist at different levels of the organisation. A danger is that lean is devolved down the management structure to the extent that senior managers lose their grasp of and enthusiasm for the process. For this reason a lean champion must be retained at a senior level if the lean initiative is to be successful.

8 Learn to ask questions

Lean is about not accepting the status quo. It is about questioning the way things are done and the efficiency with which they are carried out. It is about speed and flow, and seeking out waste and inefficiency.

Learn to ask open-ended questions. Many tools can be used

to help develop your questioning skills. The 5 Whys technique provides a simple starting point. It involves asking why something is done the way it is, and the response to the answer is to ask 'Why?' a further four times to drill down to the fundamentals of the process and to tease out any bottlenecks and problems. The 5 Whys is a fundamental component of root cause analysis.

9 Map processes – value stream tools

There are many tools and techniques in the lean toolbox, but value stream mapping (VSM) is one commonly used in lean transformation.

In a VSM activity teams come together to record, analyse and improve flow in a value chain. This is a powerful tool that quickly helps you to see how different activities contribute towards adding value, or act as blockages to the delivery of the product or service.

The aim of a VSM activity is to:

- understand how current processes work (called current state analysis or 'as is').

- create an improved plan of how the process will work (called future state or 'to be')

- develop an implementation plan that will take you from the current state to the future state.

The organisation-wide use of VSM can help you start to see how your organisation could be organised along product family lines.

10 Understand waste

Awareness of waste, in its various forms, is a key part of lean. Waste or *muda* can be found in any activity that takes up resources but creates no value.

The philosophy of the Toyota Production System is to attain cost reductions through the elimination of wasteful operations. Taiichi Ohno, the chief production engineer who pioneered the lean production system at Toyota, identified seven types of waste:

- overproduction
- transporting
- unnecessary stock on hand
- producing defective goods
- waiting (idle/non-productive time)
- processing itself
- unnecessary motion.

Other forms of waste include:

- *mura* or waste due to variation
- *muri* or waste due to overburdening or stressing the people, equipment or system.

Sometimes the disengagement of people is identified as a form of *muda*.

Waste is relatively easy to identify in physical areas, such as parts, inventory, material and people who are not working. But it is much harder to recognise in transactional areas. Are people sitting in front of their computers adding value? Is the computer programme they are running adding value? Is the process that is consuming the results of that programme adding value? Are the data providing value?

The keys to eliminating waste are first to find it, and second to make sure that everyone recognises it as waste.

11 Recognise that lean requires constant learning

In a lean enterprise, learning and continuous improvement are fundamental parts of every job role. Although certain work skills require specialist external training, acquiring and refining lean process and improvement skills should become a regular and routine part of everyday work.

As a manager you should avoid:

- focusing on processes rather than attempting to understand customer value
- failing to get senior management support
- not engaging the workforce
- being complacent about the effectiveness of existing activities
- thinking that lean is a quick fix
- applying traditional management, accounting and operations systems to a lean environment
- moving waste within a process rather than eliminating it
- providing inadequate training for staff in the appropriate lean tools and techniques.

Supply chain management

Supply chain management is the management of the movement of goods and the flow of information between an organisation, its suppliers and its customers to achieve strategic advantage. Supply chain management covers the processes of materials management, logistics, physical distribution management, purchasing and information management. The term logistics is sometimes used synonymously with supply chain management.

This checklist describes some of the main elements in supply chain management. It focuses on business analysis, supplier management, and partnerships and networks.

Supply chain management is an effective tool for improving business processes. It begins with the source of supply and ends at the point of consumption. Supply chain management covers the flow of materials and information from suppliers, through a number of value-adding processes and distribution channels to the customer.

The aim of supply chain management is to achieve a balance between the goals of high-quality customer service and low inventory and unit cost. It is concerned with a range of issues, including purchasing, the physical movement of materials, materials management, manufacturing management and supplier management.

If properly managed, supply chain management will improve customer service, achieve a balance between costs and service, reduce costs throughout the supply chain, improve relationships between buyers and suppliers, and provide competitive advantage to all the organisations in the supply chain. Supply chain management fails if power is retained and wielded by one organisation in the supply chain, strategic fit is lacking and management styles are incompatible, or if there is a lack of willingness to cooperate for the benefit of all.

Action checklist

1 Gain an understanding of the marketplace

An understanding of the business environment is needed to determine where the supply chain management strategy can be applied to best effect. Identify the market characteristics of each product or service. Consider:

- customer needs
- pressures from suppliers
- levels of competitor activity.

Carry out a SWOT (strengths, weaknesses, opportunities, threats) analysis. Look at your current position and consider what other organisations are doing to compete on quality, service, delivery and value.

2 Analyse your business

Summarise and review the existing core competences of the organisation. What business are you in? Which operations are core to the operation and which could be outsourced?

Combine information on customer needs and strategic priorities to identify business areas where integrated supply chain management could be beneficial.

Analyse where you sit within the supply chain. Who are your suppliers and customers? Do you have good relationships with them? What level of cooperation currently exists?

3 Analyse your existing supplier base

Produce a list of suppliers for each product area. Evaluate them against a set of performance criteria. These might include price, reliability, responsiveness, delivery arrangements, use of quality systems and product specification.

How many suppliers do you need? Many organisations use far too many suppliers. The main reasons for this are:

- the belief that single-sourcing is risky
- poor supplier performance leading to a search for alternatives
- a growth in demand that cannot be met by an existing supplier
- the idea that competition among suppliers keeps the price down.

Relying on a small number of suppliers can result in a high level of dependence on them with a consequent loss of independence for the business. By contrast, using too many suppliers increases the task of controlling and managing them and raises the associated administrative costs. Reducing the number and moving towards single-sourcing can produce such benefits as:

- lower administration costs
- more time to manage each supplier
- an improvement in relationships with suppliers
- more responsive problem solving, resulting from a greater understanding of difficulties and requirements
- better communication.

When considering the number of suppliers, it is important to weigh the pros and cons and find a balance that works well for your organisation.

4 Categorise your suppliers with the aim of reducing the overall total

Having listed your suppliers and assessed them according to performance criteria, you can categorise them according to their performance level. This will help you identify preferred and strategic suppliers. Aim to work with each category of supplier to bring cost reductions to your business and to the supply chain.

Underperforming suppliers are unlikely to bring improvement ideas to the supply chain. Each represents a cost in terms of negotiation time and servicing. A substantial reduction in their number will free up time to spend on more productive supplier activities.

Enter into negotiations with preferred suppliers to explore the potential to reduce inventory, distribution, handling and warehousing costs. Cost transfers may be negotiable in return for commitments to longer-term supply.

Give consideration to your customers. Are you a preferred supplier or a strategic supplier to them? Have you discussed inventory, distribution, handling and warehousing costs with them? Have you been offered a commitment to long-term supply?

5 Investigate supply chain partnerships

The development of partnerships is a natural next step in the evolution of the supply chain. Partnerships allow organisations to work together to take advantage of market opportunities and to respond to customer needs more effectively than they could in isolation. Partnering means:

- sharing risk with others and trusting them to act in joint best interests

- a strategic fit between partners so that objectives match and action plans show synergy

- finding complementary skills, competences and resources in partners

- sharing information that may previously have been considered privileged or confidential

- involving suppliers at the earliest stages in the design of a new product.

Start with a particular supplier with which you already have a good relationship, or an emerging, forward-looking supplier. Identify a partnering champion within your organisation – someone at senior level who will become responsible for laying the foundation of the partnership and making it work in the start-up phase.

The actions needed to move towards a partnership include:

- inviting participation to improve relationships and find mutual cost benefits

- encouraging partners to put forward ideas that will benefit both parties

- starting the process of developing trust.

6 Set up a supply chain network

This involves broadening these partnerships to include your suppliers' suppliers and your customers. A process map of the entire supply chain can help. Use this map to explore total costs and movements. Does the map identify any areas of waste?

In your deliberations, remember that everyone in the supply chain needs to generate profits in order to sustain their businesses. Putting pressure on suppliers to reduce prices, rather than seeking to share the gains of cost reduction, will ultimately be counterproductive.

Gaining real commitment from all members of the supply chain means that total costs can be kept to a minimum to the benefit of everyone, so allow plenty of time for a win-win scenario to emerge. Trust takes time to develop and can be quickly lost. Each organisation is responsible primarily for its own survival, however, and cannot always put the needs of others before its own.

7 Monitor the chain

Setting up a supply chain is only the first step. Ensuring that it continues to operate as planned and delivers the benefits to all parties is critical.

Appropriate measures and indicators should be analysed regularly to ensure that everything is working to plan, so that any shortcomings can be quickly identified and action taken if necessary. For example, delivery delays could be due to short-term problems, such as a strike at a port, or potentially serious longer-term problems, such as materials shortages.

Consider the use of value stream mapping to show the parts of the supply chain where value is not added, and eliminate or reduce those elements.

Availability of timely management information associated with a carefully chosen and relatively small set of performance indicators is crucial. It should help quantify the benefits of the supply chain in terms of reduced costs, reduced delivery times, improved quality, reduced administration costs and, above all, improved customer satisfaction.

As a manager you should avoid:

- forgetting to put your own house in order first
- ignoring areas of potential conflict
- entering into partnerships without genuine commitment from senior management in each organisation.

Effective purchasing

Effective purchasing is about buying the right goods and services from the right source, at the right time, at the right price, in the right quantity and of the right quality required by an organisation to enable it to fulfil its commitments and achieve its objectives. Effective purchasing maximises efficiency and is consistent with the organisation's overall strategy.

In an age of increasing complexity and globalisation, the effective management of the supply chain has a vital contribution to make to organisational growth and prosperity. Effective procurement is not just about getting a good deal and it is not over once a purchase has been agreed or a contract signed on favourable terms. It requires constant monitoring and evaluation of the performance of suppliers and contractors as well as the service provided by the purchasing department itself.

An effective purchasing strategy can:

- add value for the organisation through efficiency and cost savings
- ensure the timely availability and quality of goods required by the organisation
- build good relationships with suppliers based on trust
- balance controls and risks in the procurement process
- support payment and accounting processes
- lead to a better understanding of the marketplace.

This checklist aims to help managers responsible for purchasing to adopt an effective strategy and to develop cooperative and mutually beneficial relationships with suppliers. It presents a proactive approach to purchasing and is intended to outline the major issues to be considered rather than provide details of the administration of purchase order processes. It is aimed at those involved in centralised purchasing, but the principles apply equally to decentralised buying, including project and contract purchases.

Action checklist – your organisation

1 Review current practice

Take the time to review how well procurement is being handled across the organisation. Are purchases completed in a timely, effective and consistent manner? How is the service provided by the purchasing function perceived? Are items being purchased by project managers at inflated prices? Do purchases meet requirements and specifications? If the answer to any of these questions is negative, you may wish to consider introducing the use of standards, such as the Chartered Institute of Purchasing and Supply's Global Standard for Procurement and Supply.

Consider what is important to each department in terms of the supply of goods and services. What are the most crucial aspects for each line or project manager in terms of quality, price and delivery? Which items do they purchase most often and what are they used for? How does each department determine its reorder levels? Gather as much data as you can to provide a sound basis for the formulation of your strategy. This will also serve to demonstrate professionalism to your internal customers and increase their sense of involvement in the process.

2 Compile a purchase history

Review purchase orders, requisitions and contracts to compile a history of purchases. Gather data on product types, order quantities, lead times, pricing and order frequency. Use this data to get a clear picture of the pattern of purchasing for key items. Pay particular attention to purchases that are incurred by one department and charged back to another.

3 Use the purchase history to become a proactive buyer

A clear understanding of the purchase history will enable you to negotiate better deals with suppliers, as you will be able to give them an indication of the volumes they can expect over the year. Anticipate reorder dates and do the groundwork in advance. Reduce delivery charges by ordering similar products at the same time. Arrange for suppliers to stock frequently used items free of charge, thus reducing your storage requirements, controlling lead times and giving the benefit of bulk purchasing. Monitor price fluctuations for seasonal trends.

4 Define and communicate your strategy

Make sure that your procurement strategy is clearly defined and communicated to all managers and directors. Consider whether decentralised arrangements could be helpful, weighing increased risks against potential cost and efficiency improvements. Set out your budget targets for the year ahead and the improvements that are required in areas such as order handling and efficiency. Devise an action plan for implementation and ensure that the targets are built into individual and departmental objectives.

Action checklist – your suppliers

1 Evaluate potential suppliers and undertake a risk analysis

Find out all you can about potential suppliers. Undertake company searches and review company accounts and annual reports. Examine their websites, browse information on products and services, and ask to see samples where appropriate. Take up references and try to identify buyers in organisations similar to your own who can give feedback on supplier performance.

Areas to cover include:

- turnover and profitability
- how long the company has been trading
- who the major customers are
- whether the company is reliant on one major customer and what might happen if this account is lost
- what percentage of their turnover your business will generate
- who their manufacturers are and where they are located
- whether the company has any third-party certification, such as ISO 9000
- standard terms of trading and warranties
- terms relating to deliveries, shipments and services
- quality control policy
- ethical and environmental policies and practice
- procedures for handling customer complaints
- invoicing and administrative procedures
- levels of insurance cover.

To ensure the resilience of the supply chain, a risk analysis of suppliers should be carried out. No supplier can be guaranteed to deliver 100% of the time. Once information has been gathered, an assessment of the risks against prioritised requirements is essential.

2 Visit potential suppliers

Visit the suppliers wherever possible, and ask for a tour of their premises, including the works and warehousing facilities. Find out who would be dealing with your orders and how they would be processed. Ask to meet the people with whom you would have day-to-day contact.

3　Develop positive relationships

Developing constructive relationships with your suppliers will help to ensure that you get the best deals and the best service. View your suppliers as partners and treat them with respect. Take an interest in your suppliers' business and anything that may affect their performance. Have they won or lost any major contracts? How are they affected by the economic situation? Will transport costs increase if fuel prices rise? Will the price of paper materially affect a major print job scheduled for the end of the year? Take account of any challenges or difficulties they face and be prepared to help where possible. Can you pre-purchase goods to minimise the effect of price rises, for example? Find out about their areas of expertise and take advantage of their specialist knowledge. They may be able to obtain goods that they do not normally hold at advantageous rates.

4　Maintain good communication

Good communication is a fundamental building block of constructive business relationships. You expect your suppliers to keep you advised of delivery dates and of any problems associated with your orders, so make sure that you reciprocate – advise them if you are expecting a sudden decrease in purchases or, indeed, an increased requirement for particular items. Just as you should tell them exactly what you want of them, get them to tell you what they expect of you.

Talk to senior managers and keep in regular contact with them. Get to know those you have dealings with as human beings. It is much easier to deal with matters (especially tricky ones) when you know the person at the other end of the phone. However, do not allow personal considerations to outweigh business considerations.

5　Audit your major suppliers

Perform regular audits of your suppliers to assess their continued level of performance. Do they still meet the criteria you established when placing the first order? What improvements or deterioration in standards have you noticed in the service since then?

6 Maintain a competitive element

Conduct regular reviews of the prices and service you are getting from your suppliers. Let them understand that they have to remain competitive. Keep up-to-date with pricing and discount structures and be prepared to make suggestions that will help you get a better deal in the future. Pricing policies can be influenced by the customer, so ensure that the price you get represents good value for your organisation.

However, do not take a heavy-handed approach, dictate terms on a take-it-or-leave-it basis, or try to exploit your suppliers. Be open to negotiation. For audit purposes keep copies of documentation showing that you have sought alternative prices.

7 Compare quotations

When comparing quotes, make sure that these are based on a level playing field. Check exclusions such as delivery, installation, training and insurance. Check the contract period, renewal dates and how long the price cited will be held. In the case of long-term contracts, consider what provision has been made to hold prices at the current level or in line with increases in the retail prices index. What are the payment terms?

8 Keep up-to-date with the marketplace

Visiting trade exhibitions and reading trade journals are important ways of keeping up-to-date with the marketplace and what is on offer. Online demonstrations, presentations and podcasts are also helpful in informed purchasing. These can save a lot of time if you filter invitations carefully to identify the most relevant events.

9 Negotiate when the price must rise

If price rises are inevitable, try to negotiate other benefits, such as longer payment terms, prompt-payment discounts, quarterly as opposed to monthly invoicing, management reports, price stability for a fixed period, free delivery, or increased frequency of delivery. It may be possible to negotiate benefits even after orders have gone through and invoices have been received. Remember that the supplier wants to retain your business and may be able to help in other ways. Remember to negotiate terms for services such as maintenance.

Action checklist – general good practice

1 Establish a code of ethics

- Use the same timescales when requesting payments from your own clients as for making payments to your suppliers. Do not borrow long and lend short.

- Respect confidentiality. Do not disclose suppliers' prices and methods of trading to competitors.

- Declare any personal interest.

- Do not accept gifts from suppliers or potential suppliers. It is good practice to advise all suppliers of this in writing when you commence trading with them, especially before the Christmas period when most suppliers traditionally bear gifts.

2 Fulfil your side of the contract

Take care to place orders in good time, and make sure that they are timely and accurate and that invoices are promptly checked and payment approved by the due dates. Ensure payments are made on time in accord with your agreement and that settlement discounts are correctly and promptly deducted. If you have a roll-over contract, make sure that you know how much notice is required, should you wish to terminate the contract.

3 Maintain an audit trail

Always maintain an audit trail of all purchase documents. Use a change management system to keep track of supplier history, assumptions made and actions agreed. Check orders, invoices and deliveries to make sure that:

- supplier accounts are not incorrectly set up or modified, resulting in false payments
- orders are not made for goods that are not required
- purchase order requisitions are authentic – make inquiries if there is the slightest doubt
- excessive charges have not been made – particularly when published pricelists are not available
- invoices are matched against purchase order requisitions
- duplicate invoices are not received, resulting in duplicate payments
- automated advance payments are not made for goods or services that have not been received
- quantities received are correctly input on goods received notes
- goods received are exactly what was ordered and not cheaper substitutes
- returns and credit notes are dealt with promptly
- orders and invoices are not lost or misplaced due to incorrect filing
- all records are accurate and up-to-date.

4 Manage risks

Identify risks related to the procurement process. These include:

- overstocking and inflated inventory
- purchase of unsuitable goods or services
- shortages or misallocation of stock
- price fluctuations

- the risk of fraud through inadequate budgetary controls
- incomplete or incorrect paperwork and records
- the loss of data through computer failure
- risks associated with your company's reputation vis-à-vis suppliers and customers or clients.

Maintain a register of risks, score them at regular intervals and keep the register up-to-date.

Make sure that financial approval policy is sound, so that the purchasing manager can detect any errors or inflated charges. Effective budgetary controls that assign appropriate levels of authority to managers and other staff involved in making purchases will act as a barrier to fraud and corruption. Weak budgetary controls may allow fraud, for example in cases when costs have been allowed in the budget but allocated purchases are not required, when overruns are concealed or transferred, or where expenses are charged back to other departments.

As a manager you should avoid:

- allowing yourself to be dragged into a Dutch auction by suppliers
- making assumptions – make sure all details are clarified in writing
- exceeding the limits of your authority
- letting your purchasing department be perceived as delaying the purchasing process
- staying with the same supplier 'because we've always used them' – be sure they are being used because they are the best
- moving to another supplier because of a minor dispute when the existing supplier is reliable and competitive.

Inventory management

Inventory management is the total of the policies, practices and procedures an organisation follows to ensure that its stocks are balanced at levels that are consistent with both meeting predetermined standards of service and releasing funds for the purposes of working capital.

For the purposes of this checklist, strategic stock is defined as essential stock, without which the organisation cannot function. Non-strategic stock is defined as basic commodities that can be readily sourced and so are not critical to the overall function of the organisation.

A fundamental dilemma lies at the heart of inventory management, or stock control, as it is still often known. On one hand, too much stock of the wrong kind – or even the right kind – means that cash resources are tied up unnecessarily, that cash flow is prejudiced and, in extreme cases, that survival may be in jeopardy. On the other hand, too little stock of the right kind means that an organisation may be unable to meet customer needs in a timely fashion. It is clear, therefore, that a failure to manage inventory levels carefully can lead to serious problems.

Stocks are held by retailers (finished goods), wholesalers (finished goods), manufacturers (finished goods, part-finished goods, parts and raw materials), local authorities, public bodies and most other types of organisations (a range of stocks for use or distribution).

The introduction of an inventory management system requires

significant effort and resources, but it also offers maximum advantage at a reasonable cost, ensuring that:

- cash is released for the major purposes for which the organisation exists

- the standard of service is consistent with predetermined policy

- stockholding costs (the cost of finance, storage, insurance, handling, obsolescence, pilferage) are minimised.

Stockholding levels are generally determined by the lead time of stock items. If the lead time of an item is one year, more than a year's usage of that item may be required. Conversely, if the lead time is one day, a day's usage may be all that is required. This means that the focus on managing stock levels should include a focus on reducing lead times for all stock keeping units (SKUs) and reducing their number. Stock turn (value of sales divided by the value of stock) is a valuable measure of supply chain effectiveness. A stock turn above a hundred would be considered very good, and one of less than ten very poor.

Action checklist

1 Be aware of the key elements of inventory management

Inventory management can be simple, using ledger books and card-index systems. However, today it is usually carried out at a more sophisticated level, and in large organisations it can involve highly computerised operating environments. Whatever type of system you establish will need to provide information on current stocks regularly. It should also record supplies received together with sales, deliveries, outputs and usage. The system adopted will depend on common sense – the cost of the system and its operation must not be greater than the cost of the problem it is intended to solve. It will not be necessary to keep precise stock records for every item held, but the following elements must be built into any stock control system:

- identification of current stock levels
- recording of receipts/dispatches
- identification of reorder levels and quantities (by analysing lead times, volume discounts, price stability)
- establishment of a pattern of regular auditing and stock checking.

  Identifying reorder levels carries a cost in itself, in the form of higher ordering costs, possible loss of bulk discounts and possible additional handling charges.

2 Analyse usage and demand levels

Analyse usage of all items in terms of:

- volume
- strategic/non-strategic stock.

  It is important to:

- recognise products that must be available on demand and 'be right' first time
- classify products in terms of importance to overall turnover but not in big product families or in other broad product groupings
- focus attention on the items that produce the most revenue
- avoid trying to give equal attention to all stock items
- analyse sales to identify the real money earners and recognise that 50% will probably yield only 10% of the total value.

  Identify the level of stock that must be held to avoid the risk of missing important opportunities or failing to supply basic needs. Identify non-strategic stock and reduce it by means of:

- special offers
- non-replacement
- repackaging
- scrapping for salvage value
- in extreme cases, writing it off.

Do not spend time on monitoring products that yield 5–10% of annual revenue; instead, reduce your stocks of these and monitor the right 20% to achieve control over 80% of total stock values. Avoid making arbitrary demands to reduce stocks by X%, as to do so may result in reduced service levels without identifying areas of wasted investment.

The main objective is to identify the level of stock above which excess inventory ties up money and diminishes the return on capital employed.

3 Plan your stocking area

- Locate frequently used items in an accessible place.

- Train staff in methods of handling – manual handling and operation of mechanical handling equipment.

- Choose appropriate stacking methods. Consider pallets, drums, bins, shelving, pipe racks. Do not try to store every item in the same environment.

- Consider shelf life and implement a stock rotation system.

- Consider storing large or bulky items at your suppliers, if you have insufficient space. Make sure that availability meets requirements.

- Use an appropriate labelling system for stock identification (this might include barcoding or a simple handwritten label).

- Consider environmental conditions, such as temperature and humidity.

4 Establish appropriate resourcing

Do not underestimate the number or quality of staff required to run your inventory management system. Too few and you will lose control of your stocks; too many and the cost of running the system will be prohibitive.

5 Determine the cost of stockholding

Identify (if any):

- financial costs (for example, the cost of funds or lost opportunities for better investment)
- storage costs, including equipment and labour costs
- costs of protection from damp, cold or damage
- insurance costs
- handling costs
- costs of obsolescence
- cost of losses through pilferage
- the alternative rental value of your storage facilities.

6 Adopt a common-sense approach

You cannot control every item by quantity – you would not expect someone to count paperclips or screws. Consider classifying such items as consumables and make a decision not to count them. Some lines may be controlled by weight.

7 Build links to other departments

Try to develop a system which links through to other departments. A system that works hand-in-hand with the accounts department, for example, will minimise workloads for both sections. And good communication with buyers and dispatch departments will minimise the risk of staff and plant being overworked one day and having little to do the next.

As a manager you should avoid:

- holding stocks only to fill the store or warehouse
- buying speculatively
- assuming there will be no losses from pilferage, excessive waste or other form of shrinkage
- exaggerating the potential consequences of running out
- grabbing every quantity or early delivery discount offered, assuming that it is to your advantage

- letting stock-taking become an annual nightmare – do partial stock-taking regularly

- thinking that an inventory management system must be expensive and complex – a basic system may give you control that is lacking now at a cost lower than the resulting savings.

Deciding whether to outsource

Outsourcing is generally understood to mean the retention of responsibility for services by an organisation that has devolved the day-to-day delivery of those services to an external organisation, usually under a contract with agreed performance standards, costs and conditions.

In this checklist the organisation considering outsourcing some or part of its functions is called the organisation; and the external organisation that is taking them on is called the agency.

Outsourcing has evolved into a strategic option for businesses of all sizes. Often seen as a threat by employees and an opportunity by organisations, outsourcing has nonetheless become standard practice in many businesses. The scope of outsourcing deals has expanded from back-office administrative processes to include entire functional areas, such as human resources and IT.

On the surface, the benefits of outsourcing may seem both straightforward and considerable. However, as well as cost-savings, there are many other factors that lead managers to consider outsourcing. These include access to skills and new technology, the desire to expand globally and the need for flexibility, both to deal with rises and falls in product demand and to improve ways of delivering products or services.

In the early years of the twenty-first century, the focus of outsourcing moved from the transfer of business process activities to locally based third-party organisations to more global offshoring strategies, taking advantage of low-cost operations in countries such as India. Some companies, however, have encountered problems with offshoring, including falls in customer satisfaction levels and a failure to realise the expected financial gains. Experience shows that both outsourcing and offshoring have their pitfalls, risks and costs. The pros and cons of outsourcing, offshoring or keeping activities in-house need to be carefully weighed and managed, and organisations must take care to retain a strong degree of control over outsourced services.

This checklist provides an introduction to the process of making decisions on whether, what and how to outsource. It encompasses stages in the outsourcing process, leading up to drawing up and testing a contract. The main areas to address are highlighted, but further legal advice should be sought for all contractual and employment law issues.

Action checklist

1 Establish the outsourcing project team

Treat the outsourcing proposal as a project. Apply the principles of project management, especially in selecting a project leader and team, and setting up terms of reference, method of working and an action plan.

2 Analyse your current position

To make an informed decision about outsourcing, you should ideally have carried out a radical review of the organisation's processes. You do not want to outsource an activity that might be better integrated with another you regard as core. You must have a clear vision of where the business is heading and have assessed:

- the advantages to be achieved by concentrating on core services
- the minimum involvement required in operations that do not directly affect the customer
- the level of control required in respect of non-diminishing, non-productive overheads

- functions that could be managed more effectively through an external agency.

3 Pay attention to the human aspects of outsourcing

As soon as it becomes known that outsourcing is under consideration, people are likely to suffer from anxiety and uncertainty. At best their working life will transfer from one employer to another; at worst their job could be lost. It is essential to keep people at the forefront of your thinking and do what you can to minimise uncertainty and allay unnecessary fears.

4 Benchmark

Someone, somewhere is probably doing the same thing in a better way, or in the same way at lower cost. Consider identifying appropriate benchmarking partners to share information with and find out which activities they are outsourcing.

5 Analyse the risks and benefits

Think about the core activities that should be kept in-house and where outsourcing could be beneficial. The principal questions are:

- What is core to the business and its future?
- What can create competitive advantage?

Explore the risks and benefits of different outsourcing strategies, taking the nature of your business into account. Would offshoring be a cost-effective route for the business, or would outsourcing to a local partner be more beneficial? Consider whether outsourcing should become a policy for organisation-wide application to non-core areas, be used as the need arises, or not be used at all.

6 Decide what to outsource

The decision about what to outsource follows logically from the process of analysis. If you focus on identifying the core competencies of your organisation and what differentiates it and makes it unique, those areas that make up the support, administration, routine and internal servicing of the organisation will become potential areas for outsourcing.

Areas which have traditionally been candidates for outsourcing include legal services, transport, catering, printing, advertising, accounting and, especially, internal auditing and security. More recently these have been joined by human resources, IT, data processing, information processing, public relations, buildings management and training.

Employees are often transferred along with their function to the agency organisation. Obviously, this requires careful consideration and sensitivity and may have legal implications. In the UK, for example, TUPE – the Transfer of Undertakings (Protection of Employment) Regulations 2006 as amended by the Collective Redundancies and Transfer of Undertakings (Protection of Employment) (Amendment) Regulations 2014 – must be adhered to.

7 Tender the package

The tender is both an objective document detailing the services, activities and targets required and a selling document that serves to attract potential suppliers. Outsourcing should not be seen as just a question of getting rid of problem areas, as outsourcing these is unlikely to resolve the issues automatically.

Once an attractive package has been defined, send an outline specification and request for information to those agencies likely to be interested. The outline specification describes the scope of the outsourcing proposal and the timescales the organisation has in mind. The request for information is a questionnaire-type eligibility test designed to establish the level of the agency's competence and interest. The next stage is to send out an invitation to tender – a precise, detailed document spelling out what agencies should bid for.

8 Choose a partner

The tender process should be used to evaluate the facts, but there is much more to choosing an outsourcing partner than a new supplier, because it involves a customised service, agreement on service levels and a contract. At this stage the organisation will be looking for an agency with which it can share objectives and values and have regular senior management meetings, and to which it will be able to disclose otherwise confidential information. Choosing an agency whose organisational culture and management style harmonises with that of the organisation is central to the success of the relationship. The organisation should also look for:

- a proven track record, a flexible approach and financial viability
- experience in handling the sensitive issue of staff absorption
- evidence of quality management
- an understanding of how important the contract is for the agency in terms of turnover.

9 Communicate with your employees

It is important to communicate with your staff in a clear and timely manner and to explain the rationale for the decision to outsource. A range of issues will need to be addressed, including terms and conditions of employment and appropriate compensation if employment with the agency is not available or desired. Allowing concerns to be aired and questions to be asked may help to reduce potential feelings of being dumped or cast aside. However, bear in mind that glaring conflicts in style and personalities may emerge and that these can have an impact on the contractual stage. If staff are to be transferred to the agency, they must be given the opportunity to meet their prospective new employer before any contracts are signed.

10 Draw up the contract

If the project team is to draw up the contract, it will need to have a strong legal input, relating to any legislation such as the UK TUPE regulations. As a guide, the contract should cover:

- measurable service levels the agency should provide, with checks and controls to ensure these are met – perhaps via a liaison manager – and clauses including remedies or financial compensation required if they are not

- a clear demarcation of service responsibilities and boundaries so that both organisation and agency understand who is responsible for what

- ownership of equipment and hardware

- the position of staff to be transferred to the agency and details of their terms and conditions of employment in the short, medium and long term, including the provision of pensions

- an appropriate degree of flexibility and provision for changes and adjustments, for example if business volumes increase or decline substantially

- a contract term, with a review date and provision for the function to revert to the organisation if necessary

- a pilot period before the contract becomes fully operational.

Legal advice should be sought for all contractual and employment law issues.

11 Test the contract

Make sure that the contract will stand up to the rigours and complexities of the operation in practice. A period of testing and trial provides the opportunity to make adjustments before the contract is finalised and to consider the consequences were the partnership to break down.

As a manager you should avoid:

- losing control of organisational services that are outsourced
- allowing the goal of cost savings to take precedence over everything else
- thinking that outsourcing is the answer to all problems
- letting cultural or language differences become a significant risk
- outsourcing core strategic, customer or financial management functions or operations.

Remember:

- to be clear about the scope of the services to be outsourced
- to have a clear vision of what outsourcing is to achieve
- that you are outsourcing an activity, but not the responsibility for it.

Implementing a service level agreement

A service level agreement (SLA) is an agreement between a service provider and a customer that specifies the level of service to be delivered. An SLA normally focuses on services, technical information and service standards. It is the result of negotiations between the service provider and the customer regarding the needs and constraints of each side.

An SLA is usually part of a wider framework agreement, which is often referred to as the services contract or the outsourcing contract. The agreement can be an informal contract between two parties or a legally binding contract. The legal terms, if any, are included in the framework agreement.

This checklist is designed to support managers who need to draw up and implement an SLA. It draws on examples from information technology, but it may be used for agreements in other contexts, including HR and facilities services. It does not, however, cover service agreements relating to the appointment of directors.

An SLA provides a valuable baseline for outsourcing and partnership arrangements. It presents a documented understanding of the services, quality levels and responsibilities agreed by each party. SLAs can be negotiated for the delivery of services by one organisation to another, as well as for the delivery of internal services within a single organisation. They enable each party to be specific about their expectations, spelling out what is and what is not required. SLAs help maintain relationships between the parties involved because service levels and targets can be discussed in detail, agreed and set at realistic levels. With regular communication, any problems can be identified and addressed before they become serious.

An SLA provides guidance for the service provider in planning ahead for the services required and focuses attention on any costs that might be incurred by breaches in the agreement. It will also focus attention on what is important to the customer. It can motivate a provider to deliver a better and improved service and deter the delivery of poor service.

To be fully understood and used by both parties, the SLA should be clearly written and well structured. Those in the organisation who have a thorough understanding of current services, standards and costs should be involved in preparing the agreement to ensure that any new arrangements are as good as or better than the previous ones.

An SLA should not be confused with a warranty or guarantee that comes with a product or service, in which the manufacturer or provider determines the level of after-sales service that the customer can expect to receive. The customer usually has no say in the terms and conditions of warranties.

Action checklist

1 Assess the current level of service provision

Many SLAs do not start from a clean slate. They may arise because of past problems. It is as important for the user to define the minimum levels of service required as it is for the provider to assess its current – and planned – resources and the current and planned demand. It is at this stage that levels of urgency and priority should be defined. It is helpful to assess the current position in terms of the outcomes or deliverables required rather than the processes by which they are generated. There may be better ways of producing the outcomes, and, particularly if the current processes are long-standing and perhaps arcane, assessment of future service delivery should be about the benefits it offers rather than how well it adheres to a routine specified by the customer.

2 Draw up an outline agreement

An SLA should identify at least the following elements:

- purpose of the agreement
- parties to the agreement – that is, the provider and user of the service
- service to be provided – what is and what is not included
- period of the agreement, with notice periods if appropriate
- arrangements for monitoring, measuring and review
- mechanism for resolving any conflicts
- procedure/s in case of non-performance – what happens if either party fails to meet the terms of the agreement
- procedures for change control
- degree of contribution and help from the user
- lines of communication
- any charges, and insurance cover for both parties
- means of arbitration for unresolved disputes.

The main elements that both provider and user need to clarify are:

- the nature of the service to be provided and the required standards, including appropriate measures such as availability, timeliness, relevance, accuracy and format
- limits to the extent – scope, range and hours – of the service
- response times – expected and deliverable
- any exceptions to the rule
- agreed methods for monitoring and measuring.

3 Negotiate the levels of performance

Negotiated performance levels will emerge from discussions between the parties. These need to be precise, clearly stated, realistic and measurable (see point 6), so that there is no confusion.

The SLA should provide clear statements on what performance levels are acceptable and what the escalation process is if unacceptable performance levels are encountered. This process could initially involve raising the issue with more senior levels of management, but ultimately it could result in some sort of penalty for one of the parties.

4 Include change control procedures

Future-proofing the agreement is crucial, so make sure that the agreement includes an adequate mechanism for proposing and accepting changes to service levels. This change control process should be clear and precise and should cover:

- raising the changes
- assessing the changes
- implementing the changes in the SLA.

These arrangements should be an integral part of the agreement. Leaving the negotiation until changes are needed risks damaging the relationship between the parties.

5 Assess risks and contingencies

Service levels will probably be missed at times. This could result in financial loss or reputational damage, or it could affect a client. Most SLAs will have some kind of penalty clause (and organisations will have other types of insurance), but these mitigations will take time to put in place and will not solve the immediate problem.

Thus all parties to the SLA should conduct a risk assessment as part of the exercise of writing the agreement. This will allow the user to define the level of contingency and back-up required for each element of the service. For example, if your website is supplied by an external provider and the site is unavailable, what do you do? There may be financial penalties for the supplier, but this does not solve the immediate problem of no website.

6 Measure performance and monitor faults

Agree a mechanism for monitoring and measuring the actual performance of the provider against the agreed performance levels. This normally involves producing a type of management information pack which is discussed by both parties. It should also track historical performance so that trends can be easily discovered. The escalation path for any performance problems should also be specified.

To avoid continual revision and expensive renegotiation of the SLA, place the details in an annex that is a contractual document and part of the wider framework agreement.

7 Run a trial of the SLA

The introduction of an SLA is an important step and any lack of preparation or fine-tuning may have damaging consequences. A sensible approach is to have a trial run with a user group that has a clearly defined level of service need. This group should be of a size not large enough to cause widespread damage if things go wrong, but big enough to draw conclusions and make modifications for general implementation.

8 Review the SLA periodically

Resources, demands and targets will change over time. The SLA is not cast in stone and should be reviewed at least annually. It is good practice to schedule regular meetings between the customer and service provider, and to keep both sides informed about the need for amendments to the agreement. This allows issues to be resolved before they become insurmountable problems. A potential point of disagreement is turned into a powerful means of supporting the user–supplier relationship if these meetings are then able to propose or agree amendments to the SLA, based on the shared experience of operating it.

As a manager you should avoid:

- allowing the SLA to be seen as being weighted in favour of the customer

- seeing the SLA as an opportunity to cut resources – be aware that providers may require extra resourcing to meet a required level of service and this could increase the cost of provision

- forgetting to take time to understand and analyse the service being outsourced in terms of any likely peaks and troughs in demand – ensure that any agreement specified takes this into account

- overcomplicating the SLA with too many service levels, which can make it difficult to monitor and measure.

Implementing *kaizen*

Kaizen is a Japanese word that can be translated as improvement. *Kai* means change and *zen* means for the better. It may refer to continuing improvement in personal life, home life, social life and working life. Essentially, in a work context, *kaizen* is a concept focusing on continuous improvement of processes and systems and the elimination of waste. It places a special emphasis on human efforts, teamwork, communication and the involvement and empowerment of everyone in an organisation. In a *kaizen* approach, improvement is seen as a way of life and a variety of techniques and principles are incorporated into the overall culture and philosophy of an organisation.

Developed in Japanese industry during the 1950s and 1960s and introduced to the West through the publication of Masaaki Imai's book *Kaizen: the Key to Japan's Competitive Success* in 1986, *kaizen* is an approach used by organisations to develop a culture of continuous improvement. Many see building a culture that promotes the continuous evaluation and improvement of organisational processes and systems as a key component in achieving and maintaining a competitive edge. *Kaizen* has traditionally been used to introduce a programme of small improvements in efficiency that can lead to big improvements over time, and is generally low-cost. However, it may also involve a series of shorter sporadic events. *Kaizen* events result in sudden step changes in improvement and incur higher costs. *Kaizen* methods may be used in conjunction with other quality management tools such as total quality management (TQM) and, more recently, lean management approaches.

Developing a culture of continuous improvement focuses attention on improving rather than just maintaining organisational activities. Sustaining a commitment to improvement efforts is not easy, however, and many organisations find this challenging. *Kaizen* culture aims to involve and empower everyone from the most senior manager to the most junior employee to make proposals for improvements. This is not only a powerful way to improve product and service quality for customers, but it also builds morale and self-respect in employees, increases motivation and job satisfaction, and fosters creative thinking. Good communications, teamwork and an atmosphere of trust are essential to the effective implementation of *kaizen* and help employees cope with its demands. Rewards may be incorporated as part of the recognition process, but employees generally participate for the satisfaction of using their creative skills to improve the work they do and the goods and services they produce.

This checklist provides an introduction to the concept of *kaizen* and some basic guidance on implementing *kaizen* methods within an organisation.

Action checklist

1 Understand the processes involved

According to Imai, there are three principal building blocks, or keys to satisfying the customer, to be embraced under *kaizen*:

- a continually improving quality assurance system to meet customer requirements
- a continually improving cost management system to provide the product or service at a favourable price to the customer
- a continually improving delivery system to meet customer requirements on time.

These are known collectively as QCD – quality, cost, delivery.

2 Link *kaizen* to corporate objectives

Imai asserts that the three most important elements to creating the spirit of *kaizen* are senior management commitment, senior management commitment and senior management commitment. 'Without that, you had better forget the whole thing,' he says.

Kaizen is best introduced as a means of achieving business targets. Senior managers and the board should carry out a SWOT analysis on the organisation's business programme. Existing systems and structures need to be assessed for their support for cross-functional goals. Any necessary changes in terms of organisational planning and control and personnel practices should be planned. Targets should be set and commitments should be agreed and shared. A statement of commitment by senior management to cross-functional goals such as quality and cost, to the resourcing of the programme and to auditing its progress will demonstrate the commitment to *kaizen* as part of organisational strategy.

Kaizen may be introduced in organisations as a developmental step in TQM. In such cases a culture of quality may have been developed already and quality may be integrated into organisational planning. To move towards *kaizen* from this position, first evaluate:

- how successful the quality initiative has been
- whether everybody understands the importance of quality
- whether improvements made have been publicised
- employee attitudes towards quality.

3 Plan the *kaizen* programme

A well-planned programme of *kaizen* is often broken down into three segments – management-oriented, group-oriented and individual-oriented *kaizen* – representing different levels. Each segment requires particular consideration as different management and personal skills will be needed:

- Management-oriented *kaizen* focuses upon the most important strategic issues, processes and systems.

- Group-oriented *kaizen* is based upon small-group activities that use statistical tools to solve problems.

- Individual-oriented *kaizen* is based upon the assumption that each individual can work better and can contribute to the improvement process.

4 Consider using *kaizen* events

When the need to improve processes in a specific area of the business has been identified, and time is of the essence, the use of *kaizen* events can be considered.

Rapid-improvement workshops of this kind are sometimes referred to as *kaizen* blitz and point *kaizen*. They are designed to implement process changes within a short period of time, maybe just a few days or a week. They are resource-intensive, as the attendance and commitment of all the process owners and influencers are required. In some cases, a series of events requiring the expertise of a specialist consultant may be planned, perhaps over a sustained period, but bear in mind that this will incur additional costs.

Kaizen events require excellent teamwork from all those involved if they are to be successful.

5 Allocate resources

Senior management must be prepared to allocate resources. You need to appoint a director in overall charge of the project and a manager/improvement expert to implement the programme. Improvement experts, whether internal or external, should be chosen wisely, and they may be needed for a sustained period to allow the improvement teams to develop in and understand their specialist roles. Training for all employees will be required and funding must be allocated to support this.

6 Develop a training plan

Explore your employees' training requirements. An understanding of the continuous improvement process, of cross-functional working and of problem-solving techniques is a minimum requirement. Work with your HR department or a consultant to draw up a training plan.

7 Communicate with employees

Good communications are crucial to the success of *kaizen* projects, so bring representatives from all functions and levels of the organisation into the planning process. *Kaizen* is about cultural change and employee participation, and ownership is an essential part of accepting the change process. Arrange meetings, briefing sessions and newsletters to promote the objectives of *kaizen*.

8 Focus training and development on the four Ps of quality

The four Ps are as follows:

- **Process control.** This is the management of processes to ensure a consistent and reliable level of performance. You need to identify variations and their causes, and then deal with assignable causes and random variation. Undertake process design reviews, making use as necessary of the range of analytical and quality improvement techniques – flowcharts, cause-and-effect (or fishbone) diagrams, process models, audits and process capability studies.

- **Problem identification.** If the causes of process variation are not accurately understood, problems will be incorrectly identified. Consider using a range of techniques – quality systems audits, customer complaint analysis, cost of quality studies, benchmarking, departmental purpose analysis and customer and employee surveys – to identify fundamental problems.

- **Problem elimination.** Gain an understanding of problem-solving tools – Pareto diagrams, cause-and-effect diagrams, histograms, control charts and scatter diagrams. Test solutions to see that they work as intended, that problems are prevented and that fresh problems are not caused elsewhere. Implement the solution when you are sure that you have a clear understanding of the dynamics of change.

- **Permanence.** Improvement is a continuous process. You need to make sure that the changes already made stick and that improvements continue to be made. You can use processes such as policy deployment, TQM reviews and quality function deployment. Ensuring that senior managers regularly attend quality improvement group meetings helps to maintain momentum and commitment.

9 Set up a suggestion scheme

Involving employees is an integral part of individual-oriented *kaizen*. A suggestion scheme is a good way of encouraging employee contribution. Be prepared to listen to all suggestions. Give recognition to employees' efforts and offer awards based on predetermined criteria.

10 Review

Plan to review the development of the *kaizen* programme. Assess the extent to which a process-oriented culture change has been achieved. Recognise champions and consider further training as required.

As a manager you should avoid:

- forgetting that the search for improvement is never-ending
- expecting continuous improvement to be effective without a culture of empowerment.

Risk management

ISO 31000:2009 defines risk as 'the effect of uncertainty on objectives'.

Risk management can be defined as the range of activities undertaken by an organisation to control and minimise threats to the continuing efficiency, profitability and success of its operations. The process of risk management includes the identification and analysis of risks to which the organisation is exposed, the assessment of potential impacts on the business, decisions about appropriate responses to risk and the effective implementation of measures to avoid, minimise or manage the impacts of risk.

Risk is part of life. All organisations in their endeavour to introduce change face multiple risks that may hinder or prevent them from achieving their objectives and can lead to operational disruption, escalating costs, loss of market share, reputational damage, financial loss, or in the worst-case scenario, business failure. This type of risk has a negative impact and is a threat to the organisation. However, risks can also offer opportunities to embark on new business ventures, develop new products and services, increase market share and reap financial gains.

Risks may arise from internal factors relating to organisational processes, systems and people, or come from external sources ranging from natural disasters and political upheavals to changes in the economy, the marketplace or the regulatory environment. Effective risk management gives organisations a better understanding of the kinds of risks they face and their potential impact. It enables managers to make informed decisions about how to eliminate or mitigate risk. It also helps them to be better prepared to respond to negative events, developing organisational resilience and sustainability. Ultimately, organisations that manage risk well are more likely to survive and achieve their objectives at lower overall costs.

Factors in the business environment such as the pace of change, increasing uncertainty and volatility, growing complexity and globalisation highlight the importance of risk management in the twenty-first century. High-profile difficulties in the financial services sector during the first decade of the twenty-first century have also drawn attention to the shortcomings of traditional bureaucratic risk management practices and the need for a broader strategic approach to managing organisational risk. However, at a time of increasing uncertainty, volatility and complexity in the economic and business environment, it is crucial for organisations to develop and maintain efficient processes and procedures for monitoring and assessing factors that may have a negative impact on their operations, to be aware of the risks involved in new business ventures, and to handle risk in an effective and proactive manner.

This checklist focuses on the operational aspects of risk management. It aims to give managers a basic understanding of the principles of risk management and outlines a generic process for identifying and managing risk.

Action checklist

1 Understand the organisational context

Risk management should not be divorced from organisational strategy. It needs to reflect organisational priorities and be integrated into decision-making and resource allocation across the organisation. Before starting to identify and assess risks, it is therefore important to be clear about your organisation's mission, vision and objectives. This is particularly important when managing and prioritising risk.

Risk management also needs to be part of an organisation's corporate governance framework, alongside compliance and auditing functions. Senior managers and the board carry responsibility for the overall organisational framework for managing risk and must be seen to be committed to it. An organisation's ability to weather storms depends on how seriously senior managers take risk management. Senior managers should also take responsibility for defining acceptable levels of risk – the organisation's 'risk appetite' – and ensuring that this is communicated, acted on and monitored. If risk appetite is too high, the organisation will be put at risk; if it is too low, the organisation may miss out on profitable opportunities.

2 Distinguish between different types of risk

Risks can be categorised in a number of different ways. They may be the result of internal factors such as failure to follow health and safety procedures, employee theft or fraud; or they may come from external sources, such as natural disasters, economic instability, or changes in government policies and legislation. They may be predictable or they may be completely unexpected, such as the 'black swan' events identified by Nassim Nicholas Taleb in his eponymous book, or UNK-UNKs – unknown unknowns. They may be preventable, for example inefficient processes, or unavoidable, as in the case of natural disasters. They may be wholly negative in their impact, or, as with the risks inherent in the development of a new product, they may carry the potential for financial rewards and increased market share. Different types of risk need to be handled in different ways.

When assessing organisational vulnerabilities, it is important to be aware that the risks to which an organisation is exposed will depend on its size, the nature of its activities and the sector in which it operates. Companies in the pharmaceutical industry, for example, face risks related to the handling of hazardous substances which are irrelevant to many service-sector organisations.

3 Identify risks and potential causes

Every aspect of an organisation's operations involves risk, so it is important to take a broad overview. Areas to focus on include:

- physical assets – buildings, equipment, machinery
- workplace health and safety – working conditions, hazards, including dangerous substances
- IT and telecommunications systems – robustness, security
- intellectual property – including patents and trademarks
- people – allegations of discrimination, loss of key people, inadequate training, difficulty in recruiting employees with the right skills and knowledge, cases of bullying or harassment
- supply chain – problems with suppliers, transport disruptions, customer complaints
- financial risks – cash flow and liquidity, currency fluctuations, poor returns on investment
- regulatory compliance – failure to comply with legislative requirements; legislative changes may also affect how the organisation does business
- strategic risks – due to changes in the marketplace or the business environment
- assumptions risk – the likelihood of forecast outcomes being wrong.

A range of methods can be used to gather information, including:

- brainstorming sessions
- interviews
- questionnaires
- the Delphi technique
- checklists

- consultation workshops
- incident investigation
- inspection
- auditing and review.

Identified risks, their causes and potential impacts should be listed and described in an organisational risk register. Remember that risks are interrelated and that a risk in one part of the organisation may have knock-on effects in other parts.

When compiling a risk register focus on identifying the principal risks to the organisation, rather than on producing a comprehensive listing of all possible risks. Excessive bureaucracy and complicated paperwork can render risk management processes ineffective and cause delays in responding to important risks. The aim is to manage risks in an effective and timely manner.

4 Analyse and evaluate risks

Ensure consistency by introducing standard criteria for measuring and prioritising risks. For each risk identified two main factors should be considered: probability and impact. The criteria should define what level of likelihood would be considered to be almost certain, moderate or unlikely, for example, and what level of impact would be considered to be minor, major or catastrophic. Once criteria have been set, a risk map or matrix can be used to rank risks as low, medium or high. This will enable you to prioritise the risks that will have the most serious effects on the organisation. Additional factors to consider are potential costs and timescales – is the risk likely to have an impact in the short, medium or long term?

A range of techniques may be used to analyse risk, including:

- failure modes and effects analysis (FMEA)
- scenario planning
- Monte Carlo method

- Ishikawa or fishbone diagrams
- business impact analysis (BIA)
- sensitivity analysis.

The results of the analysis should be added to the risk register, showing the cause, potential impact, likelihood and ranking of all identified risks.

5 Decide how to respond to risk

Effective channels for communicating risk and responding to it within agreed time periods are essential if risk management is to be robust and effective, as opposed to an exercise that looks fine on paper but fails to achieve its objectives.

The 4Ts approach to risk (tolerate, treat, transfer, terminate) is often used to categorise decisions about how to respond to risk.

Organisational responses to risk need to be proportionate to the level of risk and appropriate to the nature of the risk. As mentioned in point 1, decisions on whether to tolerate, treat, transfer or terminate risks should be in line with the organisation's stated risk appetite.

6 Take appropriate action to mitigate or eliminate risk

Once risks have been identified and prioritised, detailed plans of proposed responses can be developed, and again this should be recorded in the risk register. As well as details of proposed actions, plans should cover details of the people accountable for implementation and the resources needed, as well as timescales and performance measures. In larger organisations this may involve the development of integrated enterprise risk management (ERM), but all organisations need to consider the extent to which risk management needs to be integrated across the business.

7 Ensure compliance with regulatory requirements

Although risk management is not limited to compliance with legislative requirements, it is important to identify legislation with which the organisation must comply, to put appropriate systems and procedures in place, and to ensure that all relevant personnel are aware of the requirements. Responsibility for monitoring changes in the regulatory environment which will affect the organisation should be allocated to a suitable person or team, so the need for change can be flagged up and acted on whenever necessary.

8 Encourage a culture of personal responsibility

It is important that risk management is not seen as solely the responsibility of a single department or function within the organisation. Dedicated risk management departments have a role to play in overseeing risk management systems and processes, especially in larger organisations, but it is also important to promote positive risk management attitudes and behaviours and develop a culture of risk awareness across the organisation. Individuals should be encouraged to take responsibility for risk management at their own level.

It has been found that managers tend to underestimate risks and be overconfident about the accuracy of forecasts, especially where there is a history of success. Groupthink can also mean that significant risks are overlooked and doubtful suppositions go unchallenged. Clear communication and a no-blame culture are important here. Consider also building incentives into performance management and reward systems, so that individuals feel free to raise any issues and concerns, and ensure that reward systems do not encourage or reward maverick risk taking.

9 Monitor, review and report

Effective risk management is a continuous process, not a one-off exercise. Keep in mind that the levels and types of risk to which an organisation is exposed are subject to continual change both internally and externally. Procedures need to be in place to monitor the evolving operations of the organisation and developments in its operating environment, and to keep the board fully informed.

It is essential to put procedures in place for monitoring risk management practices, assessing their effectiveness, ensuring that they are being correctly implemented, and making any improvements and amendments that become necessary. Methods used to gather information may include inspections, incident investigations, audits and formal reviews, questionnaires and interviews, consultations and discussion.

Good risk reporting will help to ensure accountability and inform decision-making in the future. Reports should be timely, be tailored to the audience, focus on key messages and be presented in an accessible format.

As a manager you should avoid:

- creating overly complicated risk management processes
- forgetting to keep the risk register up-to-date
- getting bogged down in excessive detail
- letting risk management become an exercise which looks good on paper but fails to produce effective action
- allowing success to lessen vigilance regarding risk
- seeing all risk as negative.

Strategic risk management

Strategic risk management is the discipline of continuously analysing and assessing the internal and external risks to which an organisation is exposed, both actual and potential, with a view to strengthening strategic decision-making capabilities and planning contingencies.

High-profile failures of risk management in recent years have made the subject the topic of everyday conversations and political discussions. The collapse of investment banks Bear Stearns and Lehman Brothers in 2008, and the fatal fire and consequent ecological disaster at BP's Deepwater Horizon oil platform in the Gulf of Mexico in 2010 made headline news around the world and prompted calls for regulatory responses.

Intellectually, there has been a rapid popularisation of some relatively new concepts. A better understanding of how human cognitive biases can skew priorities and distract people from emerging risks, even among the most highly qualified and rationally minded senior management teams, has deepened our collective awareness. Also influential has been the black swan concept, popularised by Nassim Nicholas Taleb, a former financial markets trader and one of the few individuals to warn of the inherent risk in investment banks' market modelling before the 2008 crash. He emphasises that major external threats can arise suddenly, without warning, and that, as with many activities that involve human behaviour, it is impossible to create reliable models of markets.

All this has prompted much rethinking of strategic risk management. There has been a move away from treating risk management as a single specialism, and a realisation that it is unwise to rely exclusively on checklists, regulations or quantitative information to manage organisational risks. Risk must be understood and considered across the management team. Risk management must involve multi-disciplinary, in-depth discussions and scenario planning, and be closely linked to strategy development. Some business leaders adopt a still more radical approach, reconceptualising strategic risk management as a source of competitive advantage, rather than as a necessary evil.

Although checklists and procedures should not be the only tools for risk management, they can be useful resources, especially at an operational level. Important examples include procedures for handling hazardous substances, preventing occupational illnesses or minimising the risk of fraud.

It is wise for managers at all levels to have a good level of risk awareness, as this can inform career choices as well as operational and strategic decisions.

This checklist is designed to help managers think about the broader strategic elements of managing risk.

Action checklist

1 Develop a behavioural understanding of the business

It is now well understood that excellent recruitment and people management practice provides the best mitigation against internal risks, especially where high-risk posts are concerned. High standards of leadership and communication throughout the organisation underpin good risk management. Reliance on checklists and regulations is at best limited and at worst counterproductive, partly because rules cannot anticipate every scenario, and also because a climate of fear and an unthinking adherence to rules can themselves be risky.

2 Distinguish between different types of risk

It is helpful to distinguish between three different categories of risk:

- internal, preventable risks relating to performance and conduct
- calculated strategic risks such as investment in new markets
- external risks, including unexpected events, such as the Fukushima earthquake and tsunami in 2011, which had a huge impact on Japanese businesses.

Linked to this analysis, many managers find the four Ts – tolerate, treat, transfer, terminate – useful in deciding how to handle risk:

- A decision to tolerate risk might be made with regard to an uncertain political situation in a target market, for example.
- In the case of a clear internally generated risk, measures to treat the risk would be more appropriate.
- In some cases risk can be transferred by outsourcing a function to a specialist external provider with better back-up and specialist skills.
- In other cases, it would be deemed wise to terminate risk by, for example, exiting a market where the risks have begun to outweigh the anticipated gains.

3 Assess impact as well as likelihood

The collapse of Lehman Brothers and the explosion on the Deepwater Horizon oil platform could be categorised as low-probability/high-impact events. In the case of collateralised debt obligation trading by investment banks, however, it could be argued that the risk was much higher than analysts believed – a case of overconfidence and confirmation biases (see point 6). Some useful approaches have been developed to help management teams analyse and understand risks according to both their impact and their likelihood.

Companies are advised to take a strategic view of their approach to risk, or their risk appetite, as it is often called. This should cover such matters as tolerance for debt or a strategic approach to acquisitions.

4 Develop a behavioural understanding of markets

Market models based on the probabilities of games of chance where there are a known and finite number of variables have been challenged by Taleb, who argues that real markets are different in nature. Much of this behavioural understanding has already been used to inform investments on the financial markets, but the same principles apply to other types of markets. They are made up of human beings making economic decisions, sometimes individually, sometimes as a group, and can be influenced by unpredictable social or meteorological events.

5 Distinguish between risk and uncertainty

The difference between risk, which is identifiable, and uncertainty, which is unforeseen and unpredictable in scale, was usefully defined by Frank Knight, a twentieth-century economist. Traditional assessment tools such as SWOT (strengths, weaknesses, opportunities, threats) and PESTLE (political, economic, social, technological, legal, environmental) can also be used. Some managers define peripheral risk, which may grow in likelihood or potential impact, as a weak signal that should be taken into account.

6 Understand cognitive biases

It is well understood that humans as individuals and as groups can be prone to major errors of judgement explained by ingrained cognitive biases. One example is overconfidence bias, which probably explains why so many corporate mergers fail to achieve their expected gains. Another is confirmation bias, in which people pay more attention to evidence that supports their view than to that which contradicts it.

7 Build meetings structures that interrogate ideas

Given the nature of cognitive biases, it is generally risky to allow an individual or a small group to make major decisions without their ideas being tested. Many companies have established effective approaches to discuss and assess risks and to debate these thoroughly, with inquirers given licence to play devil's advocate. The principle of individual accountability is important here.

8 Integrate analysis and decision-making, without risk managers going native

Experience shows that the principles of risk management can be set out clearly, but it is difficult to maintain operational discipline. Risk assessment needs to be sufficiently close to the business to ensure a good understanding, but not so close that individual risk managers are captured by a local team that is too risk-hungry or, conversely, too risk-averse.

The best organisational approach may depend on the business context. The three major approaches involve the use of independent experts, facilitators, or embedded experts.

9 Build capacity in scenario planning

Scenario planning was developed by the Shell Oil Company in the 1960s. It was one of the few companies to have envisaged a transition from the Soviet Union to a more democratic group of countries and freer markets. Before 1989, many saw this as less likely than either nuclear war or an expansion of the Soviet empire. As a result, Shell was better placed than many companies for the opening of markets in eastern Europe in the 1990s. Scenario planning has been used to great effect by many strategic teams, often in conjunction with models to assess the likelihood and impact of likely or potential events.

10 Use good risk management as a source of competitive advantage

Organisations have varying levels of risk appetite with regard to strategic decisions, but all can improve their adaptability and resilience by following the principles outlined above. This can lead to risk management becoming a source of competitive advantage, as it helps organisations to respond to emerging threats and opportunities at a strategic level. Being a resilient organisation can result in enhanced brand image, stronger negotiating positions and many other business advantages.

As a manager you should avoid:

- overreliance on procedures or checklists to prevent accidents
- reliance on legislation relating to risk management
- striving to control everything
- neglecting low-probability/high-impact events
- managing for the most easily envisaged risk, rather than the most likely.

Spotting fraud

The UK Audit Commission defines fraud as:

The intentional distortion of financial statements or other records by persons internal or external to the organisation which is carried out to conceal the misappropriation of assets or otherwise for gain.

Fraud is not limited to the misappropriation of funds. It also includes the theft of stock, equipment or other assets, as well as, for example, false claims for payment for goods or services not delivered.

The focus of this checklist is on how an organisation, whether in the private or public sector, can put simple measures in place to prevent fraud. It is important to recognise that everyone has a role in the process of spotting and preventing fraud.

Fraud is a crime and there are many obvious advantages to spotting it. These include:

- saving money – the UK's National Fraud Agency estimated that fraud cost the private sector alone £5.7 billion in 2012

- avoiding damage to morale – no one wants to work for an organisation where fraud is rife and never investigated

- accountability – tackling fraud is one aspect of public, shareholder and stakeholder accountability.

In extreme cases, fraud has led to the total collapse of companies, leading to substantial job losses, zero-value shares, pension shortfalls, imprisonment and extreme embarrassment. If fraud is not tackled appropriately, it can seriously damage an organisation's reputation and affect the confidence of its funders, shareholders, customers and service users.

Fraud must be taken seriously and organisations should have a system set up to deal with it. This includes reinforcing messages about fraud for senior managers. The Confederation of British Industry (CBI) has reported that many directors consider the two most effective ways of preventing and detecting fraud are normal internal controls and internal audit.

Fraud is not only attempted by employees. It can be committed by external third parties acting independently, for example, by submitting invoices for bogus goods or services.

This checklist will help managers to spot and tackle fraud. There are two elements to tackling fraud:

- putting systems in place
- developing an anti-fraud culture.

Creating the right environment to tackle fraud requires a range of initiatives, some of which are difficult to evaluate but important nonetheless. In many organisations a good deal of apparently trivial fraud is accepted as the norm. Altering this perception and changing this practice can be difficult and may cause resentment.

The measures listed below are suggestions. You may already do many of the things mentioned. The key is to keep a balance between the procedures and guidelines, to work at developing a feedback culture, and to engage intelligently with the procedures and guidelines, adding value to transparency. Be a stickler for approaches to excellence.

Action checklist – putting systems in place

1 Write a fraud strategy statement

Write guidelines to help answer such questions as:

- When does pilfering become fraud?
- When do hospitality or perks become corruption?
- Can employees accept any gifts?

Without guiding principles, it is difficult for people to differentiate between what is accepted custom and practice and what is unacceptable. So set out a strategy on financial integrity.

Try to develop a separate procedure that spells out clearly:

- who is responsible for dealing with fraud
- the stages involved in raising and dealing with a concern.

2 Set up an audit committee

Larger organisations should establish an audit committee, which can be a useful way of setting the framework for fraud control. The committee should consist of senior stakeholders from different departments – people who have insight into the causes of fraud and sufficient influence to make any recommended changes stick.

It is recommended that smaller organisations seek professional advice.

The job of an audit committee is to:

- review the organisation's anti-fraud strategy
- help to design fraud prevention measures and develop a more effective fraud-prevention system
- help to investigate examples of malpractice and suggest action when they are uncovered.

The audit committee can act as a reporting line for an organisation's internal auditor. It acts as a guiding and controlling influence, a policy and strategy forum and a vehicle for accountability.

3 Tighten up anti-fraud procedures

Poorly documented procedures contribute to fraud. Make sure that procedures are clearly set out and that they are communicated and accessible to all employees.

4 Make the most of information technology

Organisations often hold large amounts of information, in particular financial information. Fraudsters are often able to perpetrate their crimes because one department does not know what the others are doing – this may give them the chance to carry out multiple fraud. Integrated and relational databases enable organisations to cross-reference information internally and with other organisations. Use information technology to share information and spot fraud at its source. Many local authorities, for example, share information about people who claim multiple housing benefits. This has proved a highly effective weapon against fraudsters.

5 Establish procedures for an effective fraud investigation

The following is based on a good practice checklist for an effective fraud investigation:

- appoint a steering officer for the investigation
- agree the target dates and key issues
- hold steering meetings to discuss progress, agree variations and identify future targets
- identify the actions required
- consider the likely outcomes, i.e. internal disciplinary action or prosecution
- if the indications appear serious, contact the police at an early stage and get their advice.

Action checklist – developing an anti-fraud culture

1 Set up internal checks and separate duties

The organisation should have in place a system of internal checks whereby more than one person is responsible for recording a transaction, approving a disbursement of funds or carrying out other activities such as purchases and sales that can affect the value of the organisation. For example, the person authorising the payment of an invoice should not be the same as the person who signs the cheque. Have more than one cheque signatory. Ensure that one person prepares electronic payments and another signs them off. These are just examples of internal checks that should be included within an organisation's internal control systems. Auditors, both internal and external, should be expected to examine the adequacy of an organisation's internal controls.

2 Ensure good management and leadership

Any initiative aimed at openness is only as good as its leaders. There may be some cynicism among employees about any new approach. They may have had experience of concerns being brushed under the carpet in the past. The message about fraud and corruption needs to come clearly from the top and be reinforced with action.

3 Make communication work

Involve your employees in discussions about fraud and listen to their views on what is right and what is wrong. Explain what fraud is and the effect it can have on their jobs and the services they provide to their customers (both internal and external):

- Make it known how seriously you treat the problem.
- If it is fraud, call it fraud when you find it.
- Use seminars, newsletters and briefing sessions to explain your commitment to tackling fraud and to report on your successes.

4 Provide additional anti-fraud training

Any new system needs to be reinforced with training. You can use training to reinforce messages about fraud and the need for vigilance and openness and to explain the way the system works. More importantly, training can help to instil new coaching and counselling skills that managers will need to handle concerns effectively.

5 Facilitate whistleblowing

It is important to open up routes through which concerns about fraud can be channelled. All employees must feel able to raise their concerns in confidence and without recrimination. They may need another channel for raising concerns in addition to their line managers – this could be the chief executive or finance officer, an employee in internal audit or, in a larger business, another named senior manager.

As a manager you should avoid:

- brushing fraud under the carpet
- being soft on fraud
- ignoring the concerns of employees – they are the ones who are most likely to spot fraud.

Internal audit

There is a clear distinction between internal and external audit. The Institute of Internal Auditors (IIA) defines internal auditing as:

An independent, objective assurance and consulting activity designed to add value and improve an organisation's operations. It helps an organisation accomplish its objectives by bringing a systematic, disciplined approach to evaluate and improve the effectiveness of risk management, control and governance processes.

Accounting scandals at the end of the twentieth century undermined public confidence in business and increased pressure on organisations to demonstrate to shareholders and other stakeholders that they have effective internal controls in place, and that their affairs are efficiently and responsibly governed. The collapse of companies such as Enron and WorldCom led to the introduction of new legislation, including the 2002 Sarbanes-Oxley Act in the US, which has implications for all companies doing business there. This has raised the profile of internal audit and highlighted the role it plays in managing risk and upholding standards of governance. The fundamental objective of internal audit is to ensure that internal controls are working effectively and that resources are being properly controlled. It is not just about financial controls, although these are extremely important; it also looks at the wider systems and processes within an organisation. Through its role as a key provider of assurance to management, internal audit helps to ensure that business objectives are met and that all business risks are appropriately managed.

Internal audit should be a continuous process offering many advantages. For example, it can:

- draw the attention of management to key business issues
- identify and minimise risks
- uncover weaknesses in the system of control
- detect instances of fraud or financial irregularities
- ensure regulatory compliance
- provide independent assurance that controls are operating satisfactorily and risks are being managed effectively
- make practical recommendations for improvement
- identify opportunities for improved efficiency
- give early notice of potential problems, allowing management to take action as necessary.

In the past twenty years internal audit has developed as a profession, and audits are now normally carried out by professionally qualified internal auditors. In public limited companies, internal auditors are directed by and report, ultimately, to the board audit committee. It is good practice to adopt a similar arrangement in limited companies.

This checklist is designed to give managers an understanding of the factors to be considered and the processes and procedures involved in the conduct of an internal audit, whether this is carried out by a dedicated internal audit department or by an external team appointed to carry out the audit.

Action checklist

1 Define objectives and scope

It is important to establish clear objectives for the audit, so that results can be measured against them. In most cases, an internal audit will focus on the operations of a defined business area.

The IIA identifies four main elements of internal audit:

- the reliability and integrity of financial and operational information
- the effectiveness and efficiency of operations
- the safeguarding of assets
- compliance with laws, regulations and contracts.

Depending on organisational needs, an internal audit may focus on any or all of these.

2 Decide on the approach to be used

Internal auditing encompasses a number of approaches, including:

- a systems approach, which focuses on a review of systems rather than individual transactions and processes
- a risk-based approach, which aims to identify the key risks involved in organisational operations and ensure that they are effectively managed.

The choice of approach will depend on the scope and objectives set for the audit.

3 Decide who is to carry out the audit

The internal audit may be carried out by a professional team from outside the organisation, a dedicated team or function within the organisation, or a combination of both.

4 Ensure support and resources

Before embarking on the audit process, it is important for those involved to understand the purpose of the audit and to be aware of what is required in terms of time and effort. To avoid unnecessary apprehension, make sure that all staff are fully briefed on the scope and aims of the audit. Emphasise that the aim is to identify areas for improvement rather than check up on people.

5 Brief the audit team

It is important for the auditor to have a good understanding of the business and its strategic objectives. Ensure that all the background information required is available before the auditor is briefed.

This might include:

- strategic or business plans
- standing orders
- articles and memorandums of association
- internal procedure manuals
- risk register or equivalent
- lists of key personnel
- organisational structure chart.

Arrange a meeting to ensure that the audit team has the information it needs. Do not make assumptions about the prior level of knowledge, even when employees of the organisation are carrying out the audit.

The aim of the meeting should be to:

- make sure that the objectives of the audit are clear
- find out how these objectives will be met
- agree a timetable and a plan of action
- check whether further information is needed.

6 Plan the audit

Plans should be drawn up by the audit team, based on the scope, objectives and priorities already established for the audit, taking into consideration the depth of audit required and the resources available. The plan should specify the controls to be examined, the audit processes and activities to be carried out, and a programme or schedule for the completion of each stage. A preliminary survey may be used to confirm the approach and identify sources of information.

7 Carry out the audit

There is a wide range of tools and techniques that the audit team can use to examine, analyse and test the systems and controls covered by the audit. These include documentation of processes, procedures and transactions, interviews, observation and statistical analysis.

8 Evaluate the results

Once evidence has been gathered, the next stage is for the audit team to evaluate the results. The evaluation should cover issues such as how efficiently controls are working, how effectively risks are being managed, whether control objectives are being met, whether assets are safeguarded and whether value for money is being achieved. It is considered good practice for the audit team to share any issues that are identified at an early stage, rather than wait until the formal report.

9 Prepare report and recommendations

A good audit report should cover four elements:

- condition – what is
- criteria – what should be
- cause – why the condition exists
- effect – the negative impact or risk arising from the condition.

The report should not just point out control weakness but also consider how improvements can be made. Recommendations should be supported by audit evidence and communicated clearly and concisely to enable management to understand the implications and take appropriate action. It is good practice for audit teams to involve management in discussions on areas for improvement and reach joint agreements on actions to be taken. This will help to gain buy-in and ensure implementation.

10 Act on the results

If no action is taken as a result of the audit, the time and resources invested in it will be wasted. Prioritise the areas of highest risk identified in the report and draw up an action plan to tackle the issues raised. Usually, internal auditors will agree a timetable for addressing these issues and will expect to see audit points closed out. They are also likely to follow them up at the next audit into the same business area.

11 Communicate the results

Keep everyone throughout the organisation fully informed of the results of the audit and of any changes that have been or are being made to strengthen procedures and processes. Bear in mind that in some cases documentation may need to be updated and training provided. Make sure that the wording of any recommendations does not point a finger of blame at any individuals, but emphasises the positive benefits of the changes.

As a manager you should avoid:

- seeing internal audit as a one-off project – it should be a continuous process of monitoring and introducing improvements
- failing to communicate the purpose and benefits of internal audit throughout the organisation – it may be perceived as a threat by employees who may think that it is an exercise in fault finding.

Kurt Lewin

Change management and group dynamics

Introduction

Kurt Lewin (1890–1947) was a social psychologist whose extensive work covered leadership styles and their effects, the development of force field theory, group decision-making, the unfreeze-change-refreeze change management model, the group dynamics approach to training (especially in the form of T-groups) and the action research approach to research. Lewin has had a great influence on research and thinking on organisational development, and was behind the founding of the Research Center for Group Dynamics in the US, through which many famous management thinkers passed.

Life and career

Lewin was born in Germany in 1890. In 1909 he enrolled at the University of Freiberg to study medicine, but then transferred to the University of Munich to study biology. Around this time he became involved in the socialist movement. His doctorate was undertaken at the University of Berlin, where he developed an interest in the philosophy of science and encountered Gestalt psychology. He got his PhD in 1916, while he was serving in the German army. In 1921 he became professor of philosophy and psychology at Berlin University and started to make a name for himself in publishing and teaching.

Lewin went to the US in 1933 to escape the worsening political situation in Germany. He taught at Cornell School of Home Economics and then at University of Iowa in 1935, becoming professor of child psychology at the latter's Child Research Station. In 1944 he founded, with Douglas McGregor and others, a Research Centre for Group Dynamics at the Massachusetts Institute of Technology (MIT). At the same time, Lewin was engaged in a project for the American Jewish Congress in New York – the Commission of Community Interrelations. From his work with community leaders and group facilitators in 1946 the notion of T-groups emerged. He and his associates got funding from the Office of Naval Research to set up the National Training Laboratories in 1947 in Bethel, Maine. However, Lewin died of a heart attack in 1947 before the laboratories were established.

Key theories

Leadership styles and their effects

With colleagues Ronald Lippitt and Ralph White, Lewin studied the effects of three different leadership styles on boys' activity groups in Iowa (1939). These styles were classified as democratic, autocratic and laissez-faire. Lewin found that in the group with an autocratic leader, there was more dissatisfaction and behaviour became either more aggressive or apathetic. In the group with a democratic leader, there was more cooperation and enjoyment. Those in the laissez-faire group showed no particular dissatisfaction, though they were not particularly productive either.

Significantly, when the respective leaders were asked to change their styles, the effects for each leadership style remained similar. Lewin's aim was to show that the democratic style achieved better results. The possibility of social and cultural influences undermines his finding to some extent, but the studies nevertheless suggested the benefits of a democratic style in a US context. They also showed that it is possible for leaders and managers to change their styles, and to be trained to improve their leadership and adopt appropriate management styles for their situation and context.

Force field theory

Lewin's force field theory viewed people's activity as affected by forces in their surrounding environment, or field. He defines a field as the totality of coexisting facts that are conceived of as mutually interdependent.

Three main principles of force field theory are that:

- behaviour is a function of the existing field
- analysis starts from the complete situation and distinguishes its component parts
- a concrete person in a concrete situation can be mathematically represented.

Force field theory is used extensively for the purposes of organisational and human resource development to help indicate when driving and restraining forces are not in balance, so that change can occur.

The force field analysis technique can be used to help distinguish whether factors within a situation or organisation are driving forces for change or restraining forces that work against desired changes. Examples of driving forces might be impulsions such as ambition, goals, needs or fears that drive a person towards or away from something. Lewin viewed restraining forces as different in nature, in that they act to oppose driving forces rather than comprise independent forces in themselves.

The interplay of these forces creates the stable routine of normal, regular activities, which Lewin described as 'quasi-stationary processes'. In day-to-day situations, the driving and restraining forces balance out and equalise to fluctuate around a state of equilibrium for an activity. Achieving change involves altering the forces that maintain this equilibrium. To bring about an increase in productivity, for example, changes in the forces currently keeping production at its existing quasi-stationary levels would be required, through taking one of two routes:

- strengthening the driving forces – i.e. paying more money for more productivity

- restraining inhibiting factors – i.e. simplifying production processes.

Strengthening the drivers would seem the most obvious route to take, but analysis would show that this could lead to the development of countervailing forces, such as employee concern about tiredness, or worry about new targets becoming a standard expectation In contrast, reducing restraining forces – through investment in machinery or training to make the process easier, for example – may be a less obvious but more rewarding approach, bringing about change with less resistance or demoralisation.

Lewin identified two questions to ask when seeking to make changes within the framework of force field theory:

- Why does a process continue at its current level under the present circumstances?

- What conditions would change these circumstances?

For Lewin, 'circumstances' has a broad meaning, covering social context and wider environment, as well as subgroups, and communication barriers between groups. The position of each of these factors represents a group's structure and 'ecological setting'. Together, the structure and setting will determine a range of possible changes that depend on, and can to some degree be controlled through, the pacing and interaction of forces across the entire field – that is, the force field.

Group decision-making

After the Second World War, Lewin carried out research for the US government, exploring ways of influencing people to change their dietary habits towards less popular cuts of meat. He found that if group members were involved in and encouraged to discuss the issues themselves, and were able to make their own decisions as a group, they were far more likely to change their habits than if they just attended lectures giving appropriate information, recipes and advice.

Lewin had an impact on a generation of researchers and thinkers concerned with group dynamics. In particular, it is argued that two ideas that emerged from field theory are crucial to an appreciation of group processes. These are as follows:

- **Interdependence of fate.** It is not similarity or dissimilarity of individuals that constitutes a group, but rather interdependence of fate. Any normal group, and certainly any developed and organised one, contains and should contain individuals of very different character. What is more, individuals who have learned to see how much their own fate depends upon the fate of the entire group will be ready and even eager to take over a fair share of responsibility for its welfare.

- **Task interdependence.** Interdependence of fate can be a fairly weak form of interdependence in many groups, Lewin argued. A more significant factor is where there is interdependence in the goals of group members. In other words, if the group's task is such that members of the group are dependent on each other for achievement, a powerful dynamic is created.

Lewin looked into the nature of group tasks in an attempt to understand the uniformity of some groups' behaviour. He remained unconvinced of the explanatory power of individual motivational concepts such as those provided by psychoanalytical theory or frustration-aggression theory. He argued that people may come to a group with very different dispositions, but if they share a common objective, they are likely to act together to achieve it. This links back to his force field theory. Interdependence (of fate and task) also results in the group being a dynamic whole. This means that a change in one member or subgroup has an impact on others.

Three-step change management model: unfreeze-change-refreeze

Lewin's change management model is linked to force field theory. He considered that, to achieve change effectively, it is necessary to look at all the options for moving from the existing present to a desired future state, and then to evaluate the possibilities of each and decide on the best one, rather than just aiming for the desired goal and taking the straightest and easiest route to it.

The model encourages managers to be aware of two kinds of forces of resistance, deriving first from social habit or custom, and second from the creation of an inner resistance to change. These forces of resistance are rooted in the interplay between a group as a whole and the individuals within it, and only driving forces that are strong enough to break the habits, challenge the interests or unfreeze the customs of the group will overcome the forces of resistance. As most members will want to stay within the behavioural norms of the group, individual resistance to change will increase as a person is induced to move further away from current group values.

In Lewin's view, this type of resistance can be lowered either by reducing the value the group attaches to something, or by fundamentally changing what the group values. He considered that a complex, stepped process of unfreezing, changing and refreezing beliefs, attitudes and values was required to achieve change, with the initial phase of unfreezing normally involving group discussions in which individuals experience others' views and begin to adapt their own.

Since Lewin's death, unfreeze-change-refreeze has sometimes been applied more rigidly than he intended, for example through discarding an old structure, setting up a new one and then fixing this in place. Such an inflexible course of action fits badly with more modern perspectives on change as a continuous and flowing process of evolution, and Lewin's change model is now often criticised for its linearity, especially from the perspective of more recent research on non-linear, chaotic systems and complexity theory. The model was, however, process-oriented originally, and Lewin himself viewed change as a continuing process, recognising that complex forces are at work in group and organisational dynamics.

T-groups

What is now known as the T-group (or training group) approach was pioneered by Lewin along with his colleagues and associates from the Research Center for Group Dynamics. Using Jewish and Black communities in Connecticut, they designed and implemented a two-week programme that sought to encourage group discussion and decision-making, where participants (including staff) could treat each other as peers. Bringing such groups of people together was, Lewin found, a powerful way to expose areas of conflict, so that established behaviour patterns could unfreeze before potentially changing and refreezing. He called these learning groups T-groups.

This training approach became particularly popular during the 1970s. Some interpreters of the method, however, have used it in a more confrontational way than Lewin may have intended.

Action research

Lewin's action research approach is linked to T-groups. Introduced during the 1940s, it was seen as an important innovation in research methods and was especially used in industry and education. Action research involves experimenting by making changes and simultaneously studying the results, in a cyclic process of planning, action and fact-gathering. Lewin's approach emphasised the power relationship between the researcher and those researched, and he sought to involve the latter, encouraging their participation in studying the effects of their own actions, identifying their own biases and working to transform relationships within their community.

Action research involved the participation of members of the community being researched and the pursuit of separate but simultaneous processes of action and evaluation. Different variations of this approach have evolved since Lewin's day, and its validity as a scientific research method for psychology is often questioned. Its strengths, however, in offering groups or communities an involving, self-evaluative, collaborative and decision-making role are widely accepted.

In perspective

Lewin is recognised as a seminal figure in social psychology, though his early death obscured his central role in the development of the managerial human relations movement. In the US and the UK (especially through the work of the Tavistock Institute of Human Relations), much subsequent management thinking and research has been influenced by Lewin's approaches and ideas. These, following in the tradition of Elton Mayo's 1920s and 1930s Hawthorne studies, underlie current thinking on organisational development and change management.

One of the most influential social scientists of the 20th century, Lewin continues to have a significant influence on contemporary psychological theory, research and practice. Scholars today frequently cite his thinking and research.

Business continuity planning for major disruptions

Disaster planning, crisis management, business continuity, disaster recovery – these are just some of the naming conventions used historically and internationally for several elements that play a part in business continuity planning. Collectively, the group of business continuity planning competencies required to respond to a threat, reinstate continuity, and then subsequently deliver full restoration is known as business continuity management (BCM).

The British Standards Institution Code of Practice for Business Continuity Management, BS 25999–1, defines BCM as:

A holistic management process that identifies potential threats to an organisation and the impacts to business operations that those threats, if realised, might cause, and which provides a framework for building organisational resilience with the capability for an effective response that safeguards the interests of key stakeholders, reputation, brand and value-creation.

Major disruptions to organisations come in many forms. Extreme weather conditions, technical failure, people-related factors such as increased unplanned absences, security breaches and supply chain incidents are all examples of events that can cause business disruption. Without pre-prepared systems, continuity and recovery plans and trained people in place, organisations can be irreversibly damaged as a consequence of business operations downtime, and the resulting suspension of the delivery of services and products to customers.

To ensure that organisations are equipped to effectively identify, manage, respond to and recover from major disruptions, it is essential that a BCM framework is in place. This checklist outlines the principal components of the framework, which collectively safeguards companies from harmful threats.

Action checklist

1 Understand the components of the BCM framework

The essential building blocks of a BCM framework consist of:

- BCM programme management – e.g. establishing elements such as programme scope, objectives, roles and responsibilities
- understanding the organisation and the impact identified threats would present
- determining the BCM strategy
- developing and implementing the BCM response
- exercising, maintaining and reviewing the BCM framework to ensure it remains fit for purpose at all times
- embedding BCM in the organisation's culture.

2 Gain support from senior management

The scope of the BCM programme needs to be determined and owned by senior managers. This ensures that the activities required to deliver and implement the programme are fully supported from the top down. It also ensures that the programme is delivered in accordance with the needs of the organisation from a strategic and operational perspective.

3 Outline the scope of the BCM programme

The scope of a BCM programme must be determined by the objectives and outputs it needs to deliver.

Considerations regarding scope may include the following:

- whether to include the core organisation only or all outsourced partners (managed services, supply chain, resellers)
- whether to include the whole organisation or just critical processes or departments within it
- whether to include all of the technical IT and telecommunications infrastructure or just critical dependencies for specific areas of the organisation.

4 Allocate roles and responsibilities

For an effective BCM programme to be achieved, roles and responsibilities must be clearly assigned and approved by senior management, and methods for reporting progress must be agreed and understood. Owners or champions for every element of the system must also be established to ensure smooth delivery and maintenance of the programme across the organisation.

5 Understand the organisation

Based on the agreed scope of the BCM programme, the impact on the operations of the organisation if pre-established threats were to materialise needs to be determined. Undertaking business impact analysis (BIA) and risk assessment activities (see below) will provide an understanding of the organisation and assist you in developing its capability to manage business continuity.

The personnel required to provide information for BIA and risk assessment activities should be carefully selected for their knowledge and expertise before embarking on a work stream of sequential individual and group exploration activities. This ensures the best use of the time contributed to the programme by all involved, as well as promoting the programme in a positive way.

5.1 *Undertake business impact analysis activities*

BIA targeted activities are conducted to:

- identify your organisation's critical products and services

- identify the critical processes and procedures that cumulatively deliver each product and service

- establish how the suspension of these activities will affect the organisation over an increasing time period (typically ranging from twenty-four hours to four weeks) – operational, strategic, financial and reputation impact are criteria commonly used to assess impact during BIA activities

- establish the organisation's maximum threshold for the suspension of these activities, i.e. the point at which continued suspension may lead to potentially serious or irreversible damage to the organisation

- establish the resources required to recover data, people-knowledge, IT systems, bespoke equipment, suppliers, etc

- establish known recovery capabilities and time frames.

All this information should be fully captured through a process of methodical questioning and, where possible, reviewing any evidence provided in support of the answers given. The information attained (along with risk assessment data) can then be presented to senior management so that BCM strategies can be agreed. This will also shape the direction of the BCM programme and the activities to be undertaken. The activities involved in undertaking a BIA and risk assessment will enable you to understand your organisation better and to build your BCM capability.

5.2 Conduct risk assessment activities

Agree the types of risk for exploration such as the loss of IT and communications or critical suppliers (as examples) with the BCM programme working group before embarking on risk assessment activities.

Conduct risk assessment activities to determine the likelihood and impact of these agreed risk types (if they materialised) in terms of fully/partly suspending the organisation, which would affect the delivery of business-critical products and services and disrupt critical processes and procedures as identified in the BIA stage (see above), such as the preparation and running of payroll.

5.3 *Consider mitigation options*

When all risk assessment activities have been undertaken and there is an understanding of the likelihood and impact of the risks materialising in relation to each critical element identified in the BIA, the next activity is to look at the mitigation options available so as to reduce their likelihood and/or impact (and resulting associated impacts on the organisation). Typically, the mitigation options are as follows:

- **Transfer** – i.e. outsource the root cause so that a third party carries the risk.

- **Reduce** – apply risk treatment techniques, such as preparing for the risk materialising by developing specific business continuity plans to recover from it.

- **Terminate** – look at re-engineering a process where certain risks are currently present.

- **Accept** – do nothing and hope the risk never materialises.

6 Determine BCM strategies

This element of the BCM programme provides the continuity strategies available for the maintained delivery of the critical products and services when major disruptions suspend or part-suspend them.

When you have established known recovery capabilities and time frames for each of these during BIA activities, the actual continuity strategies and resources required to achieve the required restoration time frames need to be agreed by senior management and subsequently documented.

Examples of BCM strategies may include the following:

- **People** – critical processes are documented and other staff members are then cross-skilled to be able to deliver them.

- **Premises** – provisions are made for alternative sites or remote working.
- **Technology** – technology infrastructure is split across multiple connected sites.
- **Information** – critical back-up data are maintained and stored remotely for prompt retrieval and loading.
- **Suppliers** – alternative stand-by sourcing channels are identified.

All approved continuity strategies should be included in business continuity and technical disaster recovery documentation.

7 Develop and implement the BCM response

This stage of the BCM programme focuses on the how, what and who, when recovering the organisation's critical operations following a major disruption. For effective recovery and continuity to take place, incident management systems need to be defined, processes created and appropriate plans written.

7.1 *Clarify the roles and responsibilities of the incident management team*

It is essential to have a clear understanding of the triggers that will invoke the incident management response, and of who will be responsible for assessing incidents and taking prompt decisions on whether the incident management team should be called upon. Members of the incident management team need to be identified and prepared to perform their roles, both as individuals and as part of a team. Duties should be allotted to each member ahead of a major incident occurring. Make sure that the protection and preservation of life is the top priority for the incident team. To ensure that this happens, integrate health and safety procedures in business continuity plans. This means that building evacuation and the provision of first aid (and potentially counselling services for staff if these are contracted) are automatically worked through as part of the incident management team's task list.

7.2 *Draw up business continuity plan(s)*

Critically, business continuity plans provide direction and support information to the incident management team to:

- recover the critical products and services within the timescales and priority order required (working within the maximum time thresholds the organisation can tolerate before potentially irreversible damage is caused)

- mobilise and direct the resources required to achieve continuity and recovery

- maintain the reputation of the organisation throughout the event through managed communications internally and externally

- engage coherently with third parties such as suppliers and/or emergency services as required

- maintain the confidence of employees through demonstrating that their well-being has been provided for and considered at all times

- present assurances to customers that business disruption is being managed professionally to restore normal services in the shortest possible time and with the minimum inconvenience.

Business continuity plans can be single documents consisting of many different sections, or standalone documents that serve a specific purpose, such as the communications plan, for example. Each plan should include a methodology detailing how the document would be invoked and accessed as part of the incident management team invocation process. It should also clearly state its purpose and scope. If the plan is one of a suite of plans, all relationships with other plans should be stated in the document along with information relating to the author and owner of each as appropriate.

Major incident communications stakeholder audiences need to be established externally as well as internally for completeness. Messages should be appropriate to each audience and consistent across all message platforms (such as customer-facing web pages) throughout the management of the recovery cycle. These communication requirements can be written as a standalone communications plan, or added as a section of a larger business continuity plan.

Business continuity plans should be self-explanatory, and avoid the use of unnecessary jargon. Sequential activities to achieve continuity and recovery should be included (to achieve the deliverables stated in the purpose and scope of the plan), with each activity pre-assigned to the individual roles that make up the incident management team. Remember that business continuity plans are only as good as the information contained within them, so they should be regularly reviewed, maintained and revised as part of business-as-usual document version control.

8 Exercise, maintain and review the BCM framework

Exercising, maintaining and reviewing the BCM framework is essential if organisations are to remain fully prepared. This can be achieved using a variety of different methodologies:

- **Testing** – where specific elements of your systems or plans are tested in isolation, such as the incident management team invocation process.

- **Discussion-based** – where instrumental groups of people are invited to workshops to walk through the business continuity plan(s) and concerns and assumptions are highlighted immediately.

- **Table top** – virtual events intended to test systems, rehearse people and exercise plans against scenarios which an organisation is known to be subject to.

- **Live** – generally conducted when the three options above cannot provide real data enabling any needs for preparedness improvements to be established. Live exercises can have a detrimental impact on the organisation if they are not controlled and implemented properly. As such it requires a greater degree of planning and control than the other methodologies.

Exercises should be performed at least annually. However, the frequency will be dictated by such things as business change, regulatory requirements, licensing requirements, supply chain agreements and so on. Maintain the framework by ensuring that plans are updated if critical services or products are changed, for example.

9 Embed BCM in the organisation's culture

It is essential to embed BCM into the organisation's everyday business operations. Make sure that all employees understand what their responsibilities are in reporting incidents, and that they feel assured that the organisation is best prepared to manage major incidents should they arise. Raising the awareness of the BCM framework across the organisation can be simply achieved by providing regular information using internal media (such as intranet, email, noticeboards) and communicating any scheduled exercises that are taking place. All employees should understand who is responsible for the implementation of the BCM framework, and an open-door policy for two-way information exchange should always be promoted.

BCM must also be incorporated into business change processes. Any changes in the way an organisation conducts its business operations, through new projects, fresh supply chain relationships, or changes to its portfolio of products and services, for example, will have implications for the effectiveness of business continuity plans – and these should be considered to ensure that the organisation remains prepared at all times.

As a manager you should avoid:

- being complacent – disasters are usually unexpected
- assuming you have thought of everything – listen carefully to comments and suggestions
- forgetting to test your plans
- letting your plans get out of date.

Acknowledgements

The Chartered Management Institute (CMI) would like to thank the members of our Subject Matter Experts group for their generous contribution to the development of the management checklists. This panel of 80 members and fellows of CMI and its sister institute, the Institute of Consulting, draw on their knowledge and expertise to provide feedback on the currency, relevance and practicality of the advice given in the checklists. A full listing of the subject matter experts is available at www.managers.org.uk/about-us/work-with-us/as-a-subject-matter-expert.

This book has been made possible by the work of CMI's staff, in particular Catherine Baker, Colleen Bihanycz, Piers Cain, Sarah Childs, Michelle Jenkins, Robert Orton, Alex Palmer, Nick Parker, Karen Walsh and Mary Wood, the Series Editor. We would also like to thank Stephen Brough, Paul Forty and Clare Grist Taylor of Profile Books for their support.

The management checklists are based on resources available online at www.managers.org.uk to CMI members to assist them in their work and career development, and to subscribers to the online resource portal ManagementDirect.

Index